ARSON

Jim O'Halloran

Published by
Duchess Promotions
599 Green Lane
Goodmayes
Ilford
Essex IG3 9RN

Printed in the U.K.
by Juniper House of Print

2nd EDITION

6/24

Dear Phyl & David

ARSON AROUND

Sorry it took so long
sending the book.
It was lovely to have
met you at the Chateau.
Hope you enjoy the read.
Kindest Regards

Jim O'Hallaran
X

To Joan and Corinne
with special thanks to Sharon and Richard for their belief in
the book and their support

A Mother's Pride

She was born in the East End, gave birth to three sons,
The proudest of mothers was she,
And as they grew older, all three were the ones
To protect her and show loyalty.

Through good times and bad times they stood by her side,
Through tragedy, danger and fire,
And always her head she could hold up with pride;
Their devotion to her would not tire.

This proud little family was steeped in tradition,
As close-knit as any could be;
Their numbers were few and those wishing admission
Were scrutinised mercilessly.

Throughout the war years she suffered in silence;
Her wounds were too many to count.
But her sons all stood tall, and showed true defiance,
No hardship they could not surmount.

They held their ground firmly, defended the Docks,
Cared for all throughout the years;
They suffered the trauma and all of the shocks
And lived through the laughter and tears.

When eventually she died, with her sons by her side,
In their sorrow they bade her farewell;
For their mother so proud could not alter the tide
Or the changes that time would foretell.

She named her sons Silvertown, Stratford and Plaistow,
Her own name, West Ham Fire Brigade,
And she knew that in time London's people would know
Of the brave role in history she played.

Ken Smith

Chapter One

'Come on Hooligan, the bells have gone!'

Jeff was shaking me vigorously. I rolled out of my bed, fumbled into my overalls and gave chase in my stockinged feet into the appliance bay, stepping into a puddle of water behind the pump. 'Sod it!' I pulled myself into the rear cab of the fire engine, still trying to organise my thoughts into some form of co-ordination. 'Where we going?' I said, half asleep.

'The Vic Dock,' shouted Jeff. 'Christ, Hooly, how you can sleep through those bloody alarm bells and lights I'll never know. You take a short course in death when you go to kip.'

'What we got?' I mumbled.

'One of the Star boats.'

I looked at my watch. 3.12 a.m.

As we sped along Prince Regent Lane, fire bells clanging, I opened the window and peered into the cold night air. An old man picked up his small dog and cradled it in his arms for protection as we passed. (It always amazed me that no matter what time we were called out in the night, there was always someone walking the streets).

We turned into number 8 gate where the PLA police officer directed us to the shed where the ship was berthed.

'Fire in the engine room,' someone shouted. By this time my head was clearing. Jeff and I rigged ourselves in proto breathing apparatus sets. We handed our name tallies to the control officer. The information on them, such as our names, station, amount of oxygen available and so on would be transferred to the main control board and he would calculate the duration of the set and the time we would be expected out. He duly marked our time in upon the board, observed us checking our CEAG lamps and waved us forward.

'Enjoy yourselves lads – I hear it's bloody hot down there.'

'Piss off,' I mumbled as we engaged our mouthpieces and nose clips. We pulled our goggles down and made our way up the gangplank on to the ship.

I felt comfortable with Jeff and had no misgivings in being paired with him as we had teamed up on many previous incidents and had developed a camaraderie between us of total trust and respect for each other's abilities. We descended into the bowels of the ship. As we neared the engine room, the heat was becoming intense. The unprotected parts of my face were stinging from a combination of heat and sweat.

Jeff tapped me on the shoulder and pointed in the direction he wanted to go. We pulled the hose along with us as we proceeded towards the entrance to the engine room. I signalled to Jeff that I wanted 'water on' before we entered. The signal was passed back through the ship by various personnel to the pump operator on the quayside. I reckoned that he would be pumping at about one hundred pounds per square inch in order to give us about fifty down here. I pushed the door inwards with the nozzle of the hose to prevent burning my hands on the red-hot metal door. We stepped over the bulkhead and into the engine room. Below water level, the throbbing of the generators and various steam valves hissing made a deafening vibrating sound on the metal structures. We had made our way about forty feet over to the port side of the room when a violent explosion from behind threw us into the side panels of the ship.

All was silent. My lungs were taking in large quantities of hot acrid air. Jesus, my nose clip was off! I pulled the spring-loaded clip apart and reapplied it to the burnt skin of my nose. I rolled myself over on to my knees and staggered to my feet. I can't hear! Christ, I'm deaf!

A sheet of oily flame obscured our original entrance to the engine room. Jeff had already realised that our exit was lost and was frantically signalling to me to follow him towards the rear of the room. We had had many lectures on the construction and layout of ships and now our knowledge was being put to the test. We knew there had to be a prop-shaft tunnel leading from the engine room to an eventual escape route. Christ, let it be big enough, I prayed to myself. The size of the tunnel varied from ship to ship; some were large enough to walk through and others were so small you had to crawl flat on your stomach.

I knew Jeff was saying something to me, but what? I swallowed hard and rubbed my ears vigorously. The distant throbbing was the first thing I heard, then the roaring of the fire behind us. Jeff pulled his mouthpiece further away from his mouth, a practice frowned upon by purists in the fire service because of the possibility of toxic gases passing the broken seal. 'Hooly, over here!' Jeff entered the prop-shaft tunnel with me in hot pursuit. Sod it! It was a crawling job – my worst fears had been realised. The tunnel was about six feet in diameter, but two and a half feet of that were taken up at the bottom by a metal walkway under which the prop-shaft ran. The bulkhead lights had failed during the blast and the tunnel was pitch black, filled with hot smoke and gases and full to floor level with stagnant oily bilge water.

By now, we had been on the ship for about twenty minutes. The heat was intense, causing the bilge water to feel warm to the touch. I was cold, hot, wet, shit scared and becoming increasingly aware of the difficulties in crawling along the shaft. The bag at the front of the BA set had to be released from the body harness and pushed in front to prevent its collapse as we proceeded. The clinking noise of the mica valves in the breathing tubes of Jeff's set were now quite audible as they alternately lifted and fell on to their caged seatings, something that had increased in rapidity with the exertion of his efforts.

'Hooly, stay with me.'

'I don't think we're going to make it, Jeff.'

'Bollocks,' came the terse reply. We edged our way forward. 'I can't see any bloody exit!' Jeff's voice had become more anxious. 'I think you're right, Jim, this is it!'

This is it? What the fuck's he talking about? I'm not going to die in this pox-ridden hole. 'Go on, Jeff, keep going.'

We seemed to be crawling into a dreamy dark labyrinth, with the noise of the generators and fire slowly abating. Our movements appeared strobic and animated. What in Christ's name am I doing here anyway? I never even wanted to be a bloody fireman.

Most kids in the Forties and Fifties dreamt about being doctors, steam engine drivers, firemen or even about playing football for the Hammers and becoming another Ernie Gregory. Not me mate. I never fancied the idea of getting burnt. A vet? Now that was something else.

I had tried numerous 'vocations' since leaving St Bonaventure's School: income tax clerk, menswear salesman, labourer – which I probably should have stuck to, being a Plastic Paddy – all to no avail. I suppose in those tender teen years, none of these positions suited the James Dean image I had illusions about. I enjoyed the labouring job, though, but was dismissed when I foolishly thumped the foreman whilst working for British Rail at Cable Street.

He had made several racist remarks about Paddies. In those days, racial jibes were usually solved that way as the Equal Opportunities and Racial Equalities Boards were unheard of. The joke was, I was born in Forest Gate. My father was the 'Paddy' – he came from Limerick.

I was now twenty-three and had been married to Joan for nearly four years. We now had the added responsibility of Corinne, our daughter, and therefore any position I was to pursue had to be financially rewarding and steady. It was May 1963.

The advert in the *Star* had glorified the possibilities of earning up to twenty pounds per week with tips. The drawbacks, the ad said, were unsocial hours. It wasn't until I was on my way back to Manor Park on the number 25 bus from the West End that the full implications of another drawback the greasy little bugger had mentioned hit me. They wanted a bloody male prostitute! Escort my foot!

The sound of the bells and the sudden jolting of the bus to a standstill in Stratford Broadway interrupted my thoughts. The two fire engines sped in front of and past the bus, heading towards Maryland Point. The bay doors of the fire station were still open. That's it! I'll be a bloody fireman!

On the 25th July, 1963 I became a member of the West Ham Fire Brigade. The hours were certainly unsocial: fifty-six hours a week, and the pay was twelve pounds per week with no tips, but at least I didn't have to flog my body. I reported for pre-training duties at Plaistow Fire Station, a sombre, single storey six-bayed building in Prince Regent Lane, Plaistow. Six recruits, including myself, had joined that day. We had already been togged out at Stratford Station, the brigade headquarters: one full fire-fighting uniform including cork helmet (black), fire tunic (not waterproof), black leggings (not fireproof), leather boots, leather belt and axe pouch, fireman's axe and one black silk square. The black silk became very useful in those days, as I was to find out, because the proto self-contained breathing apparatus sets were few and far between and usually at an incident it was first come, first served. If you didn't have a BA set you then donned the silk around your mouth and nose à la Dick Turpin and in you went. The old sweats encouraged you to get a good lungful of smoke, which, according to their beliefs, enabled you to become a good fireman. As most of them never enjoyed a long retirement, I had grave misgivings about their persuasions.

We spent about three weeks at Plaistow, then news came that two of us, myself and Brian Chillcott, a thickset blond lad, were to begin our training proper at the London Fire Brigade training centre in Southwark. We were told by the old hands that the next thirteen weeks would either make us or break us; little did I realise at the time just how close I would be to breaking during this period.

West Ham County Fire Brigade, like many others throughout England and Wales at this time, did not have its own training school, and therefore Brian and myself joined up with an odd bunch of recruits from Devon, Cornwall, Somerset and Wales. The 'foreigners', as we called them, actually lived in at the training centre for the duration, whilst we, being locals, were allowed the privilege of going home each evening.

Southwark is an old rambling Victorian structure and obviously built with horse-drawn fire engines in mind. An L-shaped drill yard with one drill tower made of wood and metal was surrounded by various other red-bricked buildings all eagerly used for the various aspects of training, including ongoing training for fireman drivers, turntable ladder operators, emergency tender crews and breathing apparatus. There was a fully operational fire station within the complex.

We got out at Borough Underground station with our kit bags loaded and made our way to the centre on foot. We reported in and were allocated lockers in one of the wings where the 'foreigners' had already been located. Buster Edwards, our squad instructor, seemed pleasant enough, I thought, as he explained the ground rules to us. He was a squat man, about five foot nine but appeared taller because of the uniform: trousers tucked into leather boots which finished just below the knee, sub-officer's undress jacket, and a peaked cap carefully designed to allow the plastic brim to lie over his forehead and level with his eyes. Looks like the bloody SS, I thought to myself. How close my assumption was became manifest over the next thirteen weeks.

The dormitories and locker rooms were spartan to say the least, whilst the classrooms weren't much better, although we would be spending the majority of our time in the drill yard using the tools of our trade along with a few clapped-out old Dennis fire engines that were just about capable of being used as pumps, their operational capabilities otherwise long since past.

The ex-servicemen in our squad found the tiresome marching, compulsory even when we went to tea breaks (or stand easy as it was called), second nature, but as we progressed through the course even they found the discipline and bull hard to take.

I'd been told by various people who were already in the service that you always get one in a squad, and it was my misfortune to be paired with him when our squad was segregated into twos. Taffy must have just scraped in height wise. I estimated that he was five foot six and not the five foot eight minimum requirement as laid down by the Home Office, but then he was probably related to the chief officer of the Welsh county brigade he came from. He weighed about fourteen stone. I can verify this because I had to carry him on my shoulders down a fifty-foot escape ladder at least twice a day during our thirteen week stint. Being short and stocky, it was very difficult to carry Taff, because you couldn't drape him around your shoulders; it was akin to carrying a fourteen-stone surfboard down the ladder. I was constantly terrified of dropping him during our carry-downs, as no safety harness was used in those days.

After our settling in period and numerous hours in the classroom learning about the equipment we would be using, it was now our turn to participate in hook ladder drill. The hook ladder was devised either by a sadist or a failed trapeze artist. It was thirteen foot six inches in length, had strings (sides) strengthened by piano wire, rounds (rungs) strengthened at strategic points and was highly varnished. The top of the ladder had fixed to it a steel shroud which housed a thirty-six inch hook, which in turn had serrated teeth and ended in a six inch bill. This hook could be released from the shroud by pulling a spring loaded pin and then locking the entire hook into a horizontal position at right angles to the ladder. The whole ladder weighed about twenty-eight pounds with most of the weight at the top. The ladder was used to ascend a building from the outside by throwing the ladder from one opening to an opening at a higher level: you climbed to the first floor, sat astride the window sill of that floor, lifted the ladder to the next floor up and ensured the hook was well and truly bedded into the sill before proceeding floor by floor to the top of the drill tower, which was seven floors high, about eighty feet. Our squad became strangely silent as Sub-Officer Edwards introduced us to the ladder; the usual Welsh banter was somewhat subdued and even the carrot crunchers were not their usual chirpy selves. Edwards demonstrated the art of scaling the building to the top with this terrifying piece of equipment and now it was our turn.

'Squad; squad 'shun,' bellowed Edwards. 'O'Halloran and Morgan, one pace forward, march.' Oh Jesus, why do we have to go first? Taffy and I stepped gingerly forward. 'Scale the building, two man hook ladders to the fifth floor,' the sub demanded. Fifth floor! Christ Almighty, that's fifty feet up.

'What about the third, Sir?' I enquired.

'What about the bleeding third floor, O'Halloran? It doesn't matter whether you fall from the third or the fifth, you're just as well bleeding dead. Carry on, as detailed – get to work.'

Surprisingly, Taffy and I made it to the fifth without incident. I should have realised that our descent would more than make up for it. I descended two floors to the third whilst Taffy had to reach the fourth, hook himself on to the steel ring at the top of the second ladder by way of a purpose-built hook belt worn round the waist and swivel his body away from the ladder, leaving his left foot on the ladder whilst his right foot dangled in space ready to guide the top hook ladder down towards me.

The sequence of events should have been that he now lifted the top ladder away from the fifth floor and lowered it down to me. Taffy's problem was that all the weight of the ladder was at the top. I could see his stubby arms shaking as he slowly proceeded to lower it.

'Don't you dare drop that bleeding ladder, Morgan,' screamed Edwards from below on the drill yard. 'I don't give a shit if you fall, just don't drop that ladder.' With these words of encouragement ringing in his ears, Taffy lost complete control. The ladder swayed slowly backwards towards him, impaling his head between the rounds. The poor sod was well and truly stuck, hooked on to the second ladder with the first hanging from his neck.

'Still,' screamed the sub-officer, which was the order to freeze, not that the Welshman could do anything else apart from shit himself. 'Don't move a muscle, Morgan. Get into the third floor, O'Halloran.'

I had already figured that one out for myself: fourteen stone and a ladder falling at fifty miles per hour directly towards me didn't stretch my mathematical prowess too much. Buster Edwards pounded his ample frame up the internal stairs, passing me on the third floor with instructions to follow him. We reached the fourth, where poor old Taff's face was by now a beautiful beetroot colour.

'That's a fucking hook ladder, Morgan, not a necklace,' spat Edwards as he grabbed the ladder and wrenched it over Taffy's ears. 'Get hold of this, O'Halloran.' I took the ladder from the sub and placed it on the sill. 'Now take your time, Morgan – turn slowly towards me and ease yourself in here.'

Taff swung into the tower and collapsed on all fours. He lifted his bloated face towards me, his eyes bloodshot from the pressure he'd endured. 'Jesus Christ, Jim, I thought I was a goner there, bloody lucky boyo, wasn't I?'

Taff's luck was to remain much the same, for the remainder of our training right up to our final pass out week.

During the next twelve weeks we studied chemistry, basic physics, mathematics, (with particular attention to capacities, volumes, velocity and frictional loss), report writing and first aid, apart from the obvious lectures on fire history, appliances, equipment, building construction and regulations.

It was now the last week of our training and the pass-out drill in front of the commander. The drill was to be reasonably easy, with Brian Chillcott, Taffy Morgan, Jed Cromer and myself as the crew. We were ordered to pitch the fifty foot escape ladder to the third port of the tower, effect a rescue by carrying-down a live body and provide a covering jet of water to the second floor. The rescue went like a dream, but then, Taffy, who had been used as the body to be rescued, was called upon to run a length of hose from the hydrant to the pump. Now, to make things easy for firemen, the seventy foot length of hose is fitted with instantaneous couplings at each end, one male, one female. The order for water on was given, but the unfortunate Welshman was still trying to connect one female coupling with another, and after several furtive attempts and audible blasphemous remarks directed at the said couplings, Taffy's anxiety was now extreme. 'Well,' yelled Edwards, which was fire brigade jargon to stop and wait for further instructions. 'Fall in behind the machine; about face!' He lowered his voice to a whisper. 'That was a bloody disaster.' We stood there, panting to get our breath back after the exertion we had been put through. Edwards walked menacingly towards us. Taff was shutting his eyes in preparation for the tirade of abuse about to descend upon him. To my amazement, the twisted face of Edwards stopped directly in front of me. His head dropped to one side, his face touching mine as he appeared to be inspecting my nostrils. He whispered, 'Have you got an erection, O'Halloran?'

The line of questioning threw me a bit and like a prat I looked down just in case. 'Me, sir? No, sir.'

He raised his voice to a frenzied pitch. 'Well you fucking well should have, because you are standing next to the biggest cunt on this drill yard!'

In spite of the drill, we all managed to pass out successfully, probably because Edwards and the hierarchy knew we wouldn't be joining their brigade.

In retrospect, I found the training extremely hard, particularly the physical aspect, and although at the time I never really appreciated the sub-officer's rudeness or manner, I now realise he was bullying us into a squad which would leave the training school totally confident in our equipment and more importantly in our own abilities, particularly with regards to team spirit and self-discipline.

Until now I had never really understood the term, 'esprit de corps'. Yes, I even had confidence in poor old Taffy, because Edwards had realised that he needed to be subjected to the bullying and abuse if he was to complete the course and become part of a team back home in Wales, ready to face the arduous and dangerous life he had chosen. I've never heard of or seen Taffy since, but I'm certain there's a brigade somewhere in Wales with a very good fireman in its ranks, probably a senior officer! Southwark to this day remains a training centre for recruits to the London Fire Brigade and is still very much the same apart from two new training towers and a particularly interesting museum. 'Foreigners', however, are no longer trained there.

Chapter Two

I reported for full firefighting duties the following Thursday, having had five days in which to recuperate. No. 1 station, Stratford White Watch, was to be my posting. The West Ham County Fire Brigade was small by some standards, with only two other stations, no. 2, Plaistow and no. 3, Silvertown, with Plaistow being the more modern of the three, having been opened on 29th October, 1931.

Stratford station was a beautiful yellow-brick Victorian building situated in the Broadway in the centre of Stratford between the town hall and the Two Puddings public house. Friday and Saturday nights used to get a bit rough with the drunks turning out of the pub and the town hall dances and honking up over the appliance room doors or actuating the outside fire call bell alarm. It was usually the watch room man's duty to wash the doors and forecourt down once they had dispersed. The station had three floors, four appliance bays and was separated into two blocks via the small drill yard. The two fire engines (the pump escape, so called because of the fifty foot wooden-wheeled extending ladder it carried, and the pump) were both housed at the front of the bayed building, but there was only enough sleeping accommodation in this part of the building for one crew; therefore, the other crew had to cross the drill yard, which was open to all the elements, in order to reach their appliance in an emergency.

'Fireman O'Halloran reporting for duty, Guv.' The watch room man, Fred, put the phone back on the console and pointed me towards the station officer's office. I thought Fred to be rather too old for a fireman and later discovered that he was non-operational and did mainly watch room duties. I knocked on the door. 'Come in.' I marched myself to the desk and stood to attention. 'Sit down, O'Halloran.' The command came from a man in his late thirties, dark hair slightly receding, of average build and about five foot ten. I removed my soft cap and sat down. 'My name's Rumford, Station Officer Rumford. Welcome to Stratford – tell me about yourself.'

I spoke for about ten minutes, extolling my virtues, particularly in education as I was about the only kid in St James's Road who managed to pass his eleven-plus exam and proceed to grammar school. I had already acquired the preconceived idea that I would be far too good academically for this bunch. Unfortunately, the one thing I hadn't been taught at St Bonaventure's was humility and, more importantly, common sense, as I was to discover in the early part of my career. He sat there impassively as I continued about Joan and Corinne, my ambitions and so on. When I had finished, he rose from his chair and walked towards the window. 'Irish, are you?'

'No sir, my father was.'

'Was?'

'Yes sir, he died in 1958.'

'Well, O'Halloran, with your name and your obvious pride in your education you are going to find that the lads will take the piss unmercifully. Your name you can't help but don't push the grammar school bit too much – you'll find it won't wash with this lot. In fact, they'll crucify you.' He walked towards the door. 'Follow me. I'll introduce you to the lads.' I followed him down the stairs and into the mess room.

'This is the new junior buck, name's Jim O'Halloran, a West Ham boy!' Unbeknown to me, being a West Ham boy was half the battle in eventually becoming part of the watch. Chris Rumford went on to introduce me to the watch individually. The mess man for the day poured me a cup of extremely strong tea. 'Now, Sub-Officer Docherty will take you under his wing. If we get a fire call, stick to him like shit to a blanket. If you can't find him, then go with one of the older hands and do exactly as they tell you. I'll be in my office, Sub.'

We finished our tea and the sub took me to the locker room. Docherty was an ex-Scots Guard, a man of some six foot, with a bald pate and ginger hair. He had a ruddy fair complexion and a soft Scottish accent. He looked as though he had been scrubbed with the regulation carbolic soap we were supplied with. As my career progressed, I found Jim Docherty to be totally honest, and although he didn't suffer fools gladly, everyone was treated with equality, be it praise or the rough end of a venomous Scots tongue. He was to be the finest officer I would serve with.

'This is your locker. When you've sorted your gear out, bring your fire gear across to the appliance bay and Fred will tell you what you're riding.'

I had nearly completed my locker storage when a small, waspish man entered in overalls, bumping (polishing) the parquet floor with a long-handled duster that had a rag soaked in polish wrapped around it. I remembered him as being introduced as Jock Nicholson, another Scot obviously.

'How d'ya get on at Soothark?'

'Found the physical side difficult, but the classwork was a doddle.' I had hardly finished the sentence when Rumford's warning flashed before me. Jock raised his eyebrows in a contemptuous manner. 'H'mm,' he blew through his nose. He turned his back and continued polishing.

That wasn't very clever, O'Halloran, I thought to myself.

Fred allocated me a position on the pump for the remainder of the watch. The day was uneventful as to shouts
(fire calls) and was taken up by drills, lectures, and station
work. I was given a bucket and some carbolic soap along
with a hand scrubbing brush and ordered to scrub the
concrete stairs that led down from the offices into the yard.
I discovered that these stairs were scrubbed by all three
watches on each tour of duty.

6 p.m. arrived and White watch were relieved by the
oncoming Blue watch. The fifty-six hour week was divided
into two days (9 a.m. until 6 p.m.), two nights (6 a.m. until
9 a.m. the following day) and two days off duty. This
system was worked between the three watches, Red, White,
and Blue.

Joan greeted me with excitement. 'How did you get on?
Did you have any fires?' She seemed really disappointed at
my response.

9 a.m. the following day, and roll-call was being taken by
the sub-officer.

'Riders today: PE, Sub-Officer Docherty, Fireman
Evans, Newbury, Nichols and O'Halloran. Pump: Station
Officer, Fireman Nicholson, Leading Fireman Roche,
Fireman Mumford. Watch Room: Fred, Mess: Fireman
Mumford, Assistant Mess: Fireman O'Halloran, appy Man:
Fireman Evans.

What in the name of Jesus is an appy Man, I thought to
myself. This could be a wind-up! 'Excuse me, Sub, what's
an appy Man?'

'Obviously you missed conscription, O'Halloran,' said
Nicholson.

'After tea, show him, will you, Evans?' said Docherty.

Evans was telling me about his brother Vic who was
stationed at Plaistow as we made our way across to the mess
room. 'They don't like to have two brothers on the same
watch or station in case of accident where they're both

injured or even killed.' The alarm bells stopped him in midstream. 'I'll show you the boiler room later, Jim.' We sprinted across the yard into the bay.

'RTA,' shouted Fred from the watch room door. He handed Rumford and Docherty the handwritten call slips with the address.

'Everyone on,' shouted Docherty. 'Off you go, Evans.'

We shot across the road directly in front of the station and turned right past St John's Church towards Romford Road and on to Forest Gate. The accident had been reported as at the junction of Capel Road, and Latimer Road. The PE was first to arrive at the scene.

'First aid box, O'Halloran,' shouted Docherty, alighting from the fire engine.

I grabbed the box and swiftly followed. Initially, I could see an articulated lorry but no other vehicle.

'At the back,' cried the lorry driver, gesticulating frantically.

'You tend to the injuries, O'Halloran, that's all I want you to do.'

The motorcyclist had obviously turned the corner at a fair rate of knots and seen the lorry too late. He had apparently tried to swerve, lost control and slid, complete with pillion rider, jamming both riders and the bike between the road surface and the back axle of the lorry.

'My back! My back!' screamed the rider of the bike.

'He's all right.' Tommy Roche had just arrived with the pump. 'Making enough bloody noise, anyway. See to the girl first, Jim, she looks more serious.' She was in her late teens, her long blond hair highlighted by streaks of matted blood, lying limply across her face.

Good, I thought, she's still breathing. Her head looked as though it was stuck to the road surface by congealed blood – crash helmets weren't required by law then. I crawled towards the back axle on my stomach. The youth was still screaming about his back. 'Easy now, mate, we'll soon have you out,' said Tom. The girl's breathing was shallow and she was cold and clammy to the touch. I pulled her eyelids back. At least the pupils were both the same size; that was a good sign that she hadn't suffered a compression injury to the skull. I checked her pulse; it was rapid but strong. She started to groan, slowly opening her eyes. 'You're all right, love, try not to move. I'm going to pinch your hand – can you feel it?'

'Yes,' she replied weakly.

'That's good, now I'm just going to pinch your backside – tell me if you can feel this.' Tommy Roche gave me a quizzical look.

'Can you feel it?' She nodded that she could. Good – no spine injury!

'Try to keep your head still, I'm going to put a bandage around it.'

I raised her head gently off the road, the warm congealed blood sticking to my hands as I placed a head wound dressing on the gaping wound at the back of her head.

'That's all right, mate, we'll take over now.' The ambulance crew continued the first aid as I slowly extricated myself from underneath the lorry.

By now, the wheels had been chocked with wooden blocks and the lorry was being slowly raised with hydraulic jacks from the emergency tender which had arrived from Plaistow. At each progression of the lift, more blocks were placed under the lorry in case of the jacks failing or slipping. The two riders were gently lifted on to stretchers and placed into the ambulance.

'Right, we'll get the lorry moved, then you and Evans can wash the road down with the hose-reel.' We pulled the reel off and proceeded as instructed.

I was to attend numerous such incidents later, but the first shout you get is the one that sticks in your mind. To

my surprise, I didn't feel sick and wasn't too horrified by
the incident; in fact, I felt a sense of deep satisfaction that
maybe, just maybe, I had helped to save someone's life. As
the years were to progress, I found carnage less acceptable,
probably because most of the RTAs involved young people
and I could of course relate to my daughter and her friends.

Apart from a small rubbish fire, the remainder of the day
passed quietly and I found out that the appy Man's duty
was to keep the coke-fired boilers clean and alight. It was
instant death if you let them go out!

Over the next few months I was to discover that the vast
majority of shouts were 'bread and butter' jobs: chimney
fires, rubbish fires, oil heaters and minor road traffic
accidents. One of the minor incidents I was to attend,
however, left a lasting impression on me. We were called to
a fire in a launderette in Green Street, Forest Gate. Upon
arrival it was discovered that the smoke from the fire had
affected the upstairs flat. A young expectant mother was
being led down the stairs into the fresh air by one of
Plaistow's crew whilst the other firemen were dealing with
the fire.

'Take this young lady into the café on the corner, Jim,
and get her a drink. The ambulance should be here in a
minute,' said the station officer.

I put my arm around the distressed woman's shoulder.
'Come on, love, let's get a cup of tea.'

The jukebox was blaring out Jerry Lee Lewis singing
'Great Balls of Fire'. That's very appropriate, I thought.

'Hey look at this, 'Arry, I told you firemen 'ad big
'elmits, didn't I?' I must have looked a right burk in full
firefighting gear. I took my helmet off and placed it on a
chair next to the comedian in the paint-splattered overalls.
'No offence, mate, you lot do a bleedin' good job.' I
acknowledged his praise with a smile, and sat down beside
the heavily pregnant woman.

'Thank God my mate's got the other kids, Christ knows what I'd 'ave done with them here as well,' she said. 'I keep telling them I can smell gas or something in that launderette.'

'How many children have you got, then?'

'Two and this one,' she said, pointing to her stomach. 'I keep saying to my husband, I wish we could get away from here, go somewhere nice, like Leigh-on-Sea, be smashin' for the kids, wouldn't it?' I nodded agreement. 'Not much chance of that anyway,' she went on, taking a deep breath and sighing.

'You never know, you might one day.' Pigs might fly, I thought, the poor cow's got no chance. She sipped her tea slowly.

'That'll be one and six mate, ta.' The fat aproned man thrust his hand forward. I put my hand into my overall pockets, knowing full well that my money was back at the station in my trousers.

'You tight bastard!' said the painter. 'That girl's just had a nasty shock.'

The sharp rebuke obviously struck the right nerve. 'Oh, yeah, that's all right, mate, forget it.'

She finished her tea and I walked her towards the ambulance. 'Thanks ever so much – you've been really nice,' she said as she entered the ambulance. 'See you!' The doors closed and I turned away.

'See You!' The words echoed in my ears. Little did I realise then that I would indeed see her again!

The weeks passed, and with the ongoing training I was becoming more proficient at some of the more difficult live rescue drills we had to carry out daily. One such drill nearly put me in hospital. I was to be the dummy (person being rescued) and had to be placed into a rescue line (rope), which secured my lower body and my chest by way of a sling. I was then to be lowered out of the third port of the tower ready to be lowered under foot to the ground. The rescuer would have the line over the sill of the tower and then down under his boot, between his heel and sole and then up into his hand, keeping his leg wedged against the sill wall with the assistance of another fireman. The rescuer would then slowly lower the line having taken up any slack first.

I now realised rather quickly that the second floor window was approaching at a fair old lick. Jesus! I'm dying! Evans and Nicholson were grinning like a pair of Cheshire cats peering over the third floor window, as they stamped on the line, jerking it to a sudden halt.

Oh God, the hemp rope snapped tight into my body, trying to strip the flesh from my bones. 'You dopey pair of sods,' I yelled as they continued to lower me slowly to the waiting arms of my 'friends' at ground level. I was not immediately released, however, as four lines of charged hose were strategically placed awaiting my arrival. I remained in my bondage and received the ensuing soaking with as much grace as possible, much to the delight of the sadists I now worked with.

I was beginning to be part of the watch at last and most of the guys were ready to accept the new recruit, save one, Jimmy Nicholson.

Chris Rumford had called me into the office and asked how the watch room training was going. Fine, I answered. Fred had been instructing me on days and I had even managed to master the complicated switchboard with its yards of telephone cable attached to each jack and numerous doll's eyes at each extension point. 'Do you feel confident enough to do a two hour stint tonight?'

'Yes, sir,' I replied eagerly.

'Well don't let me down, because I've discussed it with the watch and Jimmy Nicholson wasn't too convinced.'

The watch room man did his job until 11 p.m. and then the rest of the night watch was split into two hour shifts, each with a different person until 7 a.m. when the watch room attendant took over until 9 a.m. at change of shift. I was to do the first shift. I duly booked myself on duty in the log book at 11 p.m. and made an entry that the station was secure and that the lights had been extinguished. At midnight I ruled the page off and entered the new date and day. I gazed at the console, urging one of the doll's eyes to drop. I felt deflated. Only another hour to go and then I had to go over the yard and give Bill Mumford a shake. I started to read the *Stratford Express* to see if any of our jobs had been reported when the eye dropped and the phone rang. I rammed the jack into the hole. 'Fire Brigade, can I help you?'

'The fish shop's alight in Stratford Broadway. I'm a police officer, do you want my number?' he enquired in a thick Welsh accent.

Jesus, what is it about me and Taffys, I thought. I wrote his number down on the call slip, thinking how efficient it would make me appear. I pressed the call bell button and turned the lights on. I even remembered to actuate the appliance indicator lights, which informed the crews which appliances were required – in this case both machines, P and PE. 'Fish shop on fire, Stratford Broadway,' I shouted as I handed the call slips to the officers. I scrambled on to the back of the pump as we sped out of the station and down towards Bow bridge.

'Cook's, is it?' shouted Nicholson from the driver's seat.

'Must be,' I replied, 'that's the only fish shop I know in the Broadway.'

We pulled up outside the pie and mash shop. The pump's crew reconnoitred the building. 'No fire here, Guv, must be the other end of the Broadway.' We turned and sped off towards Maryland Point, passing the fire station once more, bells ringing and lights flashing, but we didn't pass any sodding fish shop. Slight signs of panic started to enshroud me and I swear Jock's driving was becoming somewhat erratic as he tried to throw the occasional threatening glance over his shoulder towards me. We raced around the island that housed St John's Church and after completing the second lap we pulled up on to the forecourt of the station where poor old Fred was feverishly trying to attract our attention.

'The copper called again, Guv, said it was the Portway.'

We encircled the Broadway once more and turned into West Ham Lane towards the Portway and arrived at what used to be a fish and chip shop. To say that my heart sank at the sight of the blackened interior would be an understatement. The fire was quickly extinguished by a crew strangely subdued with one prominent exception, Jock!

'I fucking well warned you, Guv'nor, didn't I?'

'Christ Almighty, O'Halloran,' screamed Rumford back in the security of his office, 'didn't you ask him where Stratford Broadway was?'

'I knew where Stratford Broadway was, Guv, but it was his bloody Welsh accent.'

'You knew! You knew! Then why didn't you follow the correct procedure and ask him *where* Stratford Broadway is. He would probably have said at the bottom of West Ham Lane, then you would have realised it wasn't the bloody Broadway he was on about.' He slammed the desk with his fist.

'But because of the Welsh accent, Portway sounded like Broadway,' I said apologetically.

'I don't give a fuck if he was a bloody Martian! You spell it back to them and confirm a street or landmark near the location. Make them repeat it again and again. Do I make myself clear, O'Halloran!' he yelled.

After that, I found myself in the constant care of the ginger screw, as Docherty was called by some of the watch. I found him to be hard but fair, and he would defend his men against any senior officer if he thought they were not being treated fairly. Like many of the older hands he had joined the fire brigade from the forces; in fact, the Andrew (Royal Navy) seemed to have been one of the main suppliers of manpower to the job. The Fire Service still has many navy traditions associated with it: the ringing of bells for stand easy, stand-down, lights out, etc., and the uniform jacket was a reefer. Docherty was, I found out, inclined to bend the brigade orders somewhat to allow an element of common sense to prevail in certain situations. This was illustrated vividly to me the first time we were called to a cat trapped in a tree. We arrived at the scene, and being the youngest and most agile of this older watch I was keen to perform some heroics to retrieve the stricken animal, but before I could even get out of the engine we had passed the tree and were making our way back to the station.

'Excuse me, Sub, but there was a cat in that tree, didn't you see it?'

He turned from the front of the cab to face me, and in that very gentle Scottish accent said, 'You've never seen a dead cat in a tree yet, laddie.' I gave his remark considerable thought and came to the conclusion that he was correct. I had never seen a dead cat in a tree! This logical assessment of situations was prevalent within the brigade, especially when we were called to a chimney fire at a four-storey block of flats. Smoke and burning embers were belching from the multiple chimney stack on the flat roof. Something was amiss as there were no irate residents requiring assistance to greet us.

'Two men to each floor,' ordered the sub. 'Knock on every door. See if they have a fire in the hearth.' We duly checked, but to no avail; it appeared nobody had a fire out of control.

'Well, some bugger's got a fire. Evans, fetch me a galvanised bucket off the pump.' We followed the sub-officer up the stairs, through the trapdoor and on to the roof. The offending chimney was glowing, erupting its debris skywards. Docherty took the bucket, turned it upside down and placed it over the chimney-pot. A wry smile formed on his face.

'Now we'll see who's got a bloody fire!'

At training school they taught us that there were three ways of dealing with a chimney fire: attacking with water from above, extinguishing or removing the hearth fire, and pushing chimney rods up the offending flue. The method now being demonstrated to me was definitely not in any of the manuals of firemanship.

After about three minutes had elapsed, a street door on the third floor burst open with some considerable force. Smoke billowed from the passage on to the landing. A middle-aged man appeared from the doorway, obviously suffering from the effects of inhaling large quantities of smoke. He was yelling to all and sundry that he considered the firemen present were a conglomeration of masturbators. Well, something like that anyway.

'There's the fire.' Docherty was pointing to the flat with an air of self-satisfaction.

Evans and I reached the stricken flat as Newbury and Nichols were pushing a pram out of the flat on to the balcony. I peered into the pram. Two very small white eyes were peering out from a face that would not have gone amiss on the Black and White Minstrel Show.

''Ere, give 'im to me, darlin'.' The elderly neighbour lifted the soot-covered baby from the pram. 'Call themselves bleedin' parents.' She gesticulated towards the couple who were coughing their lungs up. 'The bastards ought to be locked up – they're always pissed out of their brains and that dirty cow's just an old slag. I'm going to report them.'

The guv'nor looked apprehensively towards the crowd of neighbours who were gathering ominously around the entrance of the flat.

'Yeah, the poor little kids are left to fend for themselves – never in, those two, always in the Alice.' The stout woman waved her clenched fist at the parents.

'Tom, call the police, looks like it could get nasty,' said Rumford. We extinguished the fire in the sitting room which was littered with empty beer bottles and cleaned the hearth area; in fact, we left it a damned sight cleaner than when we arrived. We left the situation in the capable hands of the police.

Chapter Three

It was now 1964 and a new station was being built in Romford Road opposite the Pigeons public house. We became involved in the transferring of furniture, records and non-mobile equipment as it neared completion. Plans were well in advance even at this stage for the new station to become a divisional headquarters for the proposed new enlarged London Fire Brigade, due to be formed on the lst of April 1965.

The accommodation was far superior to that to which we had become accustomed. The watch room was awash with state-of-the-art technology and we would no longer be required to run across a freezing cold yard during the night to reach our fire engines. The new station had four bays and was obviously going to house more fire engines eventually, with the inevitable transfer of personnel from other stations.

Eventually we moved in to our new quarters along with our two fire engines. This was unexpected as we thought at least one machine would be transferred from Plaistow.

'Wonder if Godfrey will come with us,' said Bill Mumford.

Godfrey was our station 'ghost' back at the Broadway. Various sightings had been reported by the more gullible. He was supposed to be an old fireman. I must admit I never saw him, despite the lengths to which some of my colleagues went to in order to confirm his existence, such as the night someone had carefully walked halfway across the snow-covered drill yard then retraced their steps exactly by walking backwards. Soppy bastard must have got frozen!

'Too posh for him here, mate,' replied Tom, sarcastically.

It was indeed luxurious, with a large recreation room (and our old snooker table, from which I had been warned off by Chris Rumford who thought that my time would be better spent studying the manuals), a fully stocked bar for off-duty social occasions, and even a sun terrace – all this luxury and I, unbeknown, was about to be transferred.

I was no longer the junior buck as we had a new recruit, Dave Beswick, a rather well-spoken lad about twenty years old. I explained to Dave that, like myself, he would suffer unmercifully if he persisted in speaking the Queen's English. All the efforts of my old English language teacher, Mr Brosnan, were now dispelled and I had soon lapsed back into my cockney twang.

Dave was also getting all the jobs I had been delegated as the buck, which made me feel that I was now really one of the lads.

I was showing Dave the watch room and explaining some of the procedures when the duty man asked if I would take control for a time whilst he relieved himself. I was explaining the telephone console to Dave when a call came in from Plaistow on the internal line. The duty man in his wisdom had neglected to tell me that Chris Rumford had contacted Plaistow to speak to the chief officer Bert Cutting but had been told by Plaistow's duty man Ben Bolt that he was engaged on another line.

'Hello, Stratford,' I chirped.

'You wanted me,' came the reply.

'No, I didn't want you; you just called me.'

The voice on the line became agitated. 'You bloody well called me!' What's the matter with Bolty, getting out of his pram a bit, I thought.

'Don't be a prat, my light's just come up,' I retorted.

'Prat! Who are you calling a prat?' The voice had risen a few octaves.

'You, you prat.' What's the matter with Ben this morning?

The silence at the other end of the line gave me time to assimilate the voice pattern, and as he tendered the next question, the horrific realisation that this was *not* Ben Bolt dawned on one James Patrick O'Halloran!

'Do you realise who you talking to?'

'It's not Ben Bolt, is it?' I shook my head apologetically.

'You're fucking well right, it's not.' The receiver slammed down, causing me to push the phone away from my ear in order to prevent permanent deafness. Within ten minutes, my locker had been cleared out, my holdall packed, official notification of transfer papers shoved in my hand, and a van supplied to take me to Plaistow!

The van pulled into Plaistow's yard where I was greeted by a grinning bunch of my new comrades who had obviously heard through the jungle telegraph of my plight. The chief officer strode towards me, placed an embracing arm around my shoulder and said cynically, in a voice which was now unmistakably that which had been on the other end of the phone, 'You'll like it here, O'Halloran. I can keep an eye on your progress personally.'

I unpacked my gear and reported to the watch room, where an uncontrollable Ben Bolt greeted me.

'I don't think it's funny, Ben.'

He wiped a tear from his eye. 'Come on I'll take you over to the guv.'

I knocked on the door apprehensively.

'Come in.'

Station Officer Silvers sat behind his desk. He was in his late forties or early fifties, stocky, about five foot nine with thin mousy hair combed back.

'Sit down.' He pointed to the chair in front of his desk. 'So you're O'Halloran. Well, O'Halloran, my name's Silvers, but they think it's Bastard.' He pointed out towards the station complex.

I couldn't help but notice that the word 'bastard' was spat out from the side of his mouth. His bottom lip and jaw were heavily scarred, the lower corner of his mouth slightly deformed because of the injury.

'I've got a good watch here and I will not tolerate a disruptive influence. I'll be watching your progress very carefully, O'Halloran. Do you understand?' The words lisped from his mouth.

'Yes, sir,' I replied, wondering how he sustained the injury. In the line of duty, perhaps.

'Right, go and report to Sub-Officer Cross in the station office – he'll sort you out, and don't forget, O'Halloran, I'll be watching you,' he threatened.

'Sir!' I answered as I left the room.

Christ, the lads at Stratford said he was a nasty bastard and they weren't kidding. Cross allocated me to the back of the pump for the remainder of the watch.

Plaistow had four of the six bays in use with a pump, pump escape, emergency tender and a hundred foot Merryweather hydraulic turntable ladder (TL). This watch was therefore much larger than Stratford's, twenty-two in total. It was a very busy station, not only because of the close proximity of the docks but because the specialist machines attended shouts on other brigades' ground.

The watch was a good mixture of older experience, a few lads who had about four to eight years in, and a couple of youngsters, including yours truly. In fact, Daisy Woods had only recently joined. I was already known to most of the watch as we had met up at various incidents and combined training sessions.

'Nice to see you, Jim, there's some grub in the oven, help yourself.'

'Thanks, Jeff. How's Daisy settling in, then?'

'Bit like you, Hooly, except he's got ten GCEs and A levels.'

'Talks like an old tart, though,' declared the sub officer.

'Flakes out every time he sees claret as well,' said Evans's brother, Vic. 'So make sure you grab hold of him when we get our next RTA, Jim.'

'Poor bugger, I suppose you lot take the piss out of him, which doesn't really help.'

'He's got to learn that it's all part of the job – if he can't take it, he's no bleeding good to us,' said Bert Cross. The fire bells interrupted him.

'Sod it!' Vic Evans hurriedly took a chinagraph pencil from his pocket and started to scribble his name on his unfinished dinner plate. 'Put them in the oven, Bob,' he shouted to Fireman Annis, the mess man.

'That's no bleeding good,' cried Cross. 'Some bastard still managed to eat mine last week. They won't this bloody time, though.' He drew a deep breath through his mouth and spat on his dinner.

'Dirty git!' said Jeff. 'He gets worse as he gets older.'

We sped along the A13, passing over the Northern Outfall Sewer bank, one of the largest sewers in London, and into the sewage plant at Barking.

We were directed by the gate keeper to some pits that were on fire. A crust forms on top of the cesspits, stifling the gases underneath, causing a build-up, and in the hot weather they can easily be ignited, either by accident or by vandals.

The burning hole was not immediately accessible without traversing some other pits that were not involved.

'It's a long way round, Bert,' said Jeff.

'Yeah,' Cross rubbed his chin thoughtfully. 'There's some old planks over there – bring one over here.'

We inspected the scaffolding boards. 'They're a bit iffy, Bert.'

'Don't matter, bring them over here.'

'Some of the ground between appears to be solid, Sub – we probably won't need the planks,' suggested Daisy.

Bert glared at Woods. 'Thank you very much for your advice and observations, Mr Woods, just get the fucking planks down!'

'Come on, Daisy, give us a hand.' Jeff and I tied a line around one end of the plank and stood it up vertically beside the hole and, using the base as a fulcrum, lowered the plank across to the far side of the pit.

'Right, get the hose-reel off the pump and take it across, Mr Woods,' said Bert sarcastically.

Fireman Woods ventured timorously across the plank with the hose-reel.

'It doesn't appear too safe, Sub.'

'Oh doesn't it,' answered Bert, in an affected imitation of Woods's accent.

'Never mind, then, just try your best, Mr Woods.' He turned to us. 'How the hell did that great tart get through training?'

A loud crack sent the sub's head swivelling back towards the pit. 'Oh Jesus.' Daisy was now sinking at a tremendous speed into the quicksand-like mire, his fire helmet floating some feet away from his flaying arms.

'Keep still,' I yelled. 'Quick, Jeff, get another plank.'

'I'll get him,' said Bert as he started to manoeuvre slowly across the board.

'That's not going to hold two of them.'

'I know that, Jeff, but the sub knows best,' I declared sarcastically.

Fireman Woods had started to calm down by now, realising that he had stopped sinking. Bert had told him to place his arms out at right angles to his body in order to present a larger area to the surface of the excreta. He was in up to his armpits.

'My boots have come off, Sub,' he moaned as Bert made his way towards him.

'Sod your boots! I'm going to bend down on one knee, and when I do, I want you to slowly reach for my hand. Okay, nice and gentle now.'

The outstretched arms were inches apart when the silt beneath Daisy's feet moved, causing him to suddenly sink further. The ensuing panic induced a vice-like grip on to Bert's arm with the resultant, but inevitable, head first plunge by our revered sub officer into the shit.

He surfaced, spitting excrement and verbal abuse simultaneously at the junior buck. He tried to clear his mouth by wiping his sleeve across his mouth, but only added to the build-up of raw sewage.

'When you two wankers have stopped pissing yourselves, throw me a line,' he shrieked.

'Oh Christ, you get it, Jeff, I can't bloody well move,' I implored, tears streaming down my face. By now I was on my knees and doubled up with laughter.

'You dopey Irish bastard! Get the fucking line.' Bert's voice was now at falsetto pitch. Jeff made a running bowline and threw the rope to Bert.

'Two pairs of fucking boots and an 'elmet we've lost in that,' he continued as we dragged him to safety. 'Better get that stupid bastard out now.'

'Christ, you smell terrible, Daisy.' Jeff gave Woods a final tug towards the edge of the pit.

'There's *no* way you're going to sit next to me,' I said. 'You and Bert can sit in the back after we've hosed you down.'

We hosed the pair of them down. The stench was appalling. They discarded their fire gear (what remained of it), and their underwear into a salvage sheet. The two naked white bodies shivered as we continued to apply copious amounts of cold water to them. We tied the salvage sheet on to the back of the pump as our heroes sat meekly there, huddling together in a shared blanket. Apart from the occasional obscenity hurled in the direction of Jeff and myself from Bert, our return to the station was uneventful until we entered the yard.

'Christ Almighty! What's that smell?' enquired Vic Evans.

'Fuck off.' Bert pushed his way past Vic and marched off, totally naked, across the yard towards the showers, followed by the coy figure of Woods clasping the blanket around himself.

A broad grin spread over the craggy features of Vic's face. 'They didn't, did they?'

I nodded smugly.

'Couldn't have happened to a more deserving case.'

Our dinners had been ruined and duly dumped in the pig bin. It was stand easy, anyway. We tucked into our sandwiches.

Bert and Daisy entered the mess room door. Silver's nose twitched. 'What's that smell, old Evans?'

'Don't you start, Guv,' retorted Bert. He sat down next to the station officer with Woods alongside him.

'I can't stand too much of this.' Ken Smith, one of the new members of the watch, pushed his chair to one side and made a hasty retreat into the fresh air. He was quickly followed by the remainder of the watch, with the notable exception of two.

'I'm frightfully sorry, Sub, but I really did think I was going under. It wasn't entirely my fault, was it?'

Bert pivoted in his chair to face the unfortunate fireman. He was ready to explode. Then, realising the humorous side of the situation, he burst into gales of laughter, grabbed hold of Woods and planted a huge kiss on his lips, much to Woods's embarrassment. 'Well, at least you had the sense to take a witness with you, son.'

Cross was in his mid forties, about five foot ten, with a lean chiselled face. He was thin, yet muscular. Like so many he had gone into the fire service on coming out of the army. His hair was cut extremely short, although receding at the temples. He was typical of the vast majority of junior officers in West Ham: experienced, tough and excellent in practical firemanship, but lacking the motivation and academic ability to progress to the higher echelons within the brigade. He had become notorious throughout the brigade for outrageous escapades, some bordering on obscenity, whilst others could only be linked to certain phases of the moon's position.

Vic Evans was still grinning to himself as we washed the pump inside and out with detergent. The hundred foot line and salvage sheet were also washed and hung up on the drill tower, the highest in the brigade at seven floors. The sub-officer and Fireman Woods were taken off the run in order to attend Samson Street Hospital for the necessary jabs.

'Do you know what Bert did the other night,' said Vic. 'We'd just put the lights out in the dorm and in walks Bert, switches the lights back on and then parades up and down, totally naked with a piece of string tied round his old boy – said he was taking it for a walk. He's totally bloody mad.'

We were relieved by Blue watch at 6 p.m. Bert passed me on the way to his van.

'Do you want a lift, Jim?'

'No thanks, Bert, I'm going the other way – buses are pretty regular anyway.'

He put on his camouflage jacket and pulled his woollen khaki hat over his head as he got into the Ford Anglia van.

So ended my first tour of duty at Plaistow, the beginning of some of my happiest days in the service.

I alighted from the number 86 bus, which had stopped outside the Whitbread Brewery in Manor Park and made my way across Romford Road into Dersingham Avenue. Joan and I were fortunate in that we had rented number 305, a terraced house at the East Ham end. I say fortunate because my mother and grandparents were tenants of the landlord and had crossed somebody's palm enabling us to get the tenancy. Our rent was six pounds and six shillings a week, plus rates, and as my wage was only twelve pounds gross it didn't take a genius to work out that things were tight. We were more fortunate than some other youngsters in that the house had three bedrooms, the luxury of an upstairs bathroom, a long garden for Corinne to play in and an outside toilet. Corinne was three now and growing at an alarming rate, but didn't go short of goodies as her grandparents, who lived in Forest Gate and Goodmayes respectively, were always buying her clothes and toys.

Joan had worked as a shirt machinist prior to Corinne's birth and had contacted her old boss Sidney Lipman for some outside work. The pay was diabolical but it helped to maintain some independence for us.

The biggest drawback to my job was obviously the shift work, because on nights I could be away for over seventeen hours at a time. Our social life was restricted because apart from the money we didn't have a car and therefore our circle of friends tended to be within walking distance.

Joan never brought the subject up, but like all firemen's wives had to live with the fear of the possibility of an accident happening to me and would make sure that she always kissed me before I left for work, showing obvious relief when I returned. We argued a lot, mainly about money, but neither was one to sulk and we soon made up our differences. Regrettably, there were a lot of broken marriages in the service, possibly because of the shift system where in some cases if the wife was working the couple didn't see each other for days. We allowed ourselves one luxury, however, and that was a slot TV set. We had to put sixpenny pieces in a meter at the back of the set in order to view. This was an excellent idea as far as we were concerned, because we didn't have a bill at the end of the month as the money was collected by Granada.

'That walk nearly killed me today with the shopping, Jim. Good job Dad had Corinne for me.'

'I was thinking,' I replied, 'it would be nice if we had a little car.'

'Don't be bloody stupid, how can we afford a car?'

'We could let the spare room again.'

'Who to?'

'I don't know. We could advertise it in the corner shop.'

'Can't be sure who you'd get,' said Joan apprehensively.

We had let once before, to a young Irishman, Steve, who worked as a labourer but moved with his work after about a year to the Midlands.

The street door bell rang.

'I'll get it.' I opened the door.

'Hello Jim, I thought I'd pop in to see yee.' The soft Irish accent couldn't have been more welcome.

'Steve! Jesus, come in, come in.'

He sat down in front of the coal fire in the living room, rubbing his hands over the hearth. He explained that he was back in the area and looking for digs. We smiled simultaneously.

'Oh no.' He waved his hands in protest. 'I didn't mean to—'

'It's all right, Steve,' interrupted Joan, 'we were just talking about letting the room again when you rang the bell.'

Steve moved in once again with us. We managed to purchase a little red Ford Anglia van, on the book, which, according to our neighbours, took us into the Paul Getty class!

This enabled us to get out a bit and we found ourselves going to the Theatre Royal in Angel Lane, Stratford, which was one of our first passions when we were courting. All those wonderful old plays of Brendan Behan and Lionel Bart, ah, what memories. It's the only theatre I know where you're allowed to take your booze into the auditorium, and there's never any trouble. It was a great place because it brought together the locals and the West End theatregoers. Even an occasional Royal!

Chapter Four

I waved goodbye to Joan and Corinne as I got into our 'new' car to commence a tour of duty that was going to prove to be one of the most harrowing of my career. We had three shouts before we bedded down for the night. Two rubbish fires and a chimney – an average evening's work for Plaistow.

We were not disturbed again until 6.45 a.m. when the station call bells were tested with the customary six sharp rings and then the actuation of the fire bells. We assembled at 7 a.m. to be detailed station work cleaning duties. Jeff and I were mopping out the kitchen and dining room area whilst Vic was preparing the porridge, prior to frying the eggs and bacon.

The call bells went down at 7.21.

'Where we off to this time?' I asked, trying to keep myself upright in the back of the swaying cab and at the same time trying to put my fire tunic on. 'Laundrette, Green Street, Stratford's ground, Capes's made 'em four,' Vic shouted across to me. He was already putting the BA harness over his head in readiness for a quick entrance when we arrived. The request for four pumps meant that they required assistance in this instance by way of more manpower.

Another message crackled over the appliance radio. 'From Station Officer Capes at Green Street – persons reported.'

'Shit, this sounds like a goer,' said Vic as he and Jeff checked hurriedly over their sets. The Dennis fire engine screeched into Green Street from Barking Road, causing a cyclist to career on to the pavement.

'Take it a bit easier for Christ's sake, I nearly swallowed me bleedin' mouthpiece,' shouted Jeff to the driver, who was now speeding past the Boleyn football ground on the wrong side of the road and giving Bert, in the front seat, a real white-knuckle ride. As we approached the top end of Green Street we could see a plume of black smoke rising from the back of the three-storey terraced building.

'It's that same bloody launderette,' I cried.

'Can't be, surely,' replied Jeff.

'Christ! It is!' Vic dived from the appliance, pulling his goggles down, and was quickly followed by Jeff as they were directed to the back of the building by way of the café on the corner of Whyteville Road.

'They're still in there somewhere,' shouted an officer from one of East Ham's machines. I ran a length of inch and three quarter hose out, ready to be connected to our pump, and passed it to Bert, who was not in BA and had already started to climb the thirty-five foot extension ladder.

'Follow me, Jim.'

By this time, the heat inside the flat above the launderette had built up to such an intensity that the blackened windows began to crack and fall apart, showering glass on to us as we approached them.

'Fuck that! Watch yourself, Hooly.' Thick black smoke came belching out, spiralling its toxic fumes skywards.

'Water on, Smiffy,' bawled Bert. Ken opened the centrifugal pump outlet, slowly as a sudden surge of water could knock us off the ladder. He built the pressure up until he was satisfied we could work safely. Bert took a leg lock at the top of the ladder and with his axe proceeded to knock the loose glass from around the window frame. I huddled up closely behind him to avoid the falling glass.

'Watch yourself, Woodsie.' Dave, who was footing the ladder, dived for cover in the doorway of the shop.

'Foot the ladder now, Dave, Bert's going in,' I shouted. I let the hose ride over my shoulder, inching it up to Bert as he straddled the sash window, ripping his leggings on the only piece of glass he had missed.

'Bollocks.'

'Boots last time, leggings this time. You must be costing the brigade a bloody fortune.' I crashed on to the floor beside the sub. We both started coughing immediately, the thick smoke being inhaled in large gulps. Why me, Bert, I thought, why not Daisy? I guzzled another huge slice of the black stuff down. I pulled my silk from my neck and tied it around my mouth and nose. I had lost sight of Bert already; visibility was down to nil.

'This little lot's been going for hours.' I could hear Bert to the right of me.

'Watch the floor, Jim, there may be boards missing if they've burnt through.' Bert started crawling on all fours, going round the room in an anticlockwise direction, keeping close to the walls and feeling tentatively, searching hopefully for a body.

'Are you going the other way, Hooligan? For Christ's sake answer me! Where are you?'

I hadn't moved from the time my hand had first touched the soft bundle of clothes beside me. I stretched out my shaking hand once more and pulled it grudgingly downwards. Please God, just rags, only rags. I touched the tiny finger on reaching the extent of the sleeve. Oh my Christ! *No!*

'Bert.' My voice began breaking. 'Bert, quick, over here.'

He scrambled over to me and snatched the baby up in his arms, thrusting the bundle through the open window. 'Woodsie, quick, take this to the ambulance.'

Daisy scrambled up the ladder, snatched the child from Bert and frantically blew into its mouth as he descended before handing it over to the ambulance men. They continued furiously trying to revive the little body. As we gulped the fresh air into our lungs at the open window, it was all too obvious that their efforts were to no avail. The child had been dead long before we found it.

The BA crews entered the room and continued the search through the clearing smoke. Bert put his arm around me.

'Come on, son, let's go down and get some air.' We sat down on the pavement beside the pump, as the other crews brought out one dead body after another and placed them on salvage sheets. I tried hard not to let the tears well up in my eyes as I gazed at the lifeless body of the young woman. 'See you.' Her voice ran through my thoughts. All the poor sod wanted was somewhere nice for her and the kids. Jeff pulled me up off the pavement.

'Come on, Hooly, there's sod all we can do now, mate.' I shrugged, shook my head and followed our crew to assist in making up our gear before we returned to Plaistow. As we boarded the pump, the police surgeon had arrived and was only confirming that which we already knew.

The journey back was in total silence. The same thought must have been in all our minds: if only we had been called earlier, maybe, just maybe! We pulled into the yard and by now the effects of the smoke I had inhaled were taking their toll. Every time I drew breath my lungs felt as though they were being rasped with coarse grinding files. I had to breathe in short quick breaths to alleviate the searing pain.

'How you feeling, son?' queried Bert. 'We certainly copped a gutful there.' That has got to be the fucking understatement of all time, I thought.

'I think I'm going to die.' I made the statement with considerable thought to its content. 'I really do think I'm going to die,' I repeated.

'Come on, you silly bugger, a nice cup of tea and you'll feel wonderful,' said Bert.

'How long do you think that had been going?' wondered Vic.

'Bloody ages,' replied Bert. 'The copper said they were called about the same time as us.'

'Someone said a bloke tried to break in round the back with a builder's ladder before we arrived,' said Vic.

'Some of the neighbours said we took over half an hour to get there.'

'That's a load of cobblers and you know it Dave,' retorted Jeff.

'I bet a pound to a pinch of shit no bastard bothered calling the fire brigade,' declared Bert. 'They always assume someone else has done it. I would think Stratford were there in about four minutes and the way our driver performed, we were there in three from the time of call.'

'There'll be a coroner's inquest – it'll all come out there,' said the guv'nor wearily. 'Make sure you do an inventory on the machines, check if we've left anything there and clean the BA sets up before you go off duty.' He rose from the mess table and made his way to the office to write up his report.

'Cheer up, you two.'

Vic and I looked up at Jeff.

'Not a lot to be cheerful about,' I replied.

'You would have been smiling if you could have seen me and Vic in the back room of the flat. We were paddling in water as soon as we got in through the window; thought

Stratford had flooded the bloody place. It wasn't until the
smoke started to clear that we realised we were paddling up
and down in the bath.' I tried to smile but the effort was
half-hearted. I felt angry with our human limitations, apart
from the sheer frustration and futility of it all. The depressed mood had descended like a blanket on the entire
watch and very little was said.

Daisy, Jeff and myself made our way across the yard to
our cars at the change of watch. I looked across the roof of
my Anglia at the vacant expression on Dave's face.

'Funny thing, Jim, I have a tendency to feel sick at the
more gruesome jobs, but I didn't this morning. I just can't
get the picture of the kiddies' toys lying around the room. I
can't believe it; it seems so unreal.' Tears began to fill his
blue eyes. 'I'm sorry, Jim.' He wiped his anorak sleeve
across his face.

'Don't be, Dave. Even some of the hard bastards like
Bert were choked today. They try to put a tough image on
but they're just as gutted.'

'Yeah,' he sniffed hard, trying to hold back his emotions.

'It's times like these when you need the nutters around
to cheer the lads up.'

'Drive carefully, Jim, see you tonight.'

As I passed the Boleyn pub, I glanced down Green
Street, not that I could see anything as the job had been at
the far end. The gleeful chatter of the children queuing
outside the Odeon cinema for Saturday morning pictures
made me feel even more morose thinking of what kind of
life those poor little kids might have had if they had lived.
No Saturday morning pictures for them now, no going to
the fair at Wanstead Flats, no fishing for tiddlers with a jam
jar and net in the lake at the sandhills, no tying two knock-
ers together on street doors and running away, nothing, just
bloody *nothing!*

The sudden application of the brake lights by the Triumph Mayflower in front jolted my imagination back to reality. I slammed my brakes down hard, causing the old girl to wobble to a halt. The old Ford Anglias weren't noted for their road-holding qualities. I turned left off the Barking Road and made my way home.

'I've just heard the news. Did you go to Green Street?' Joan kissed me on the lips and I nodded my involvement.

'Did you have any breakfast?' she asked.

'No, but don't do any, not just yet anyway. Where's Corinne?'

'Dad's over, he's just taken her to the corner shop. We're going to Mum's for lunch.'

Corinne came running into the passage, arms outstretched, ready to be lifted and swung round. She giggled loudly as I cuddled her close to me. Joan joined the embrace. Nothing was said; nothing needed to be said – we were cuddling our little girl.

★

Percy, my father-in-law, a small, thin, wiry man, who had seen active service with the Middlesex Regiment, was watching me intently after our lunch.

'What's up son? Getting to you, is it?'

'I just keep thinking about it – can't get the bloody pictures out of my mind.'

'You're going to see a lot more of that in your job, son. The sooner you accept it the better.'

'It's easy for you to say that, Dad, you're a lot older than Jim, and he wasn't in the army, anyway.' Good old Amy. My mother-in-law wouldn't have a word said against me.

On our way home we passed the newspaper hoardings: 'FAMILY OF FIVE DIE IN FIRE'.

Chapter Five

I had now reached the stage in my career where I was to be trained in the use of breathing apparatus.

The BA chamber at Plaistow was primitive in the extreme. It was at the back of the yard and entered by way of two huge blackened steel doors. Some concrete steps led to a basement area below ground level which, in turn, had blackened reinforced concrete walls. The only other exit was by way of a hinged steel trapdoor which gave access to a council school field some twenty yards beyond our station's boundary wall.

The chamber itself was filthy black, with years of carbon build-up on the walls from the numerous fires burned inside. There were no extractors, making the heat and smoke, which was usually of a highly toxic nature due to the types of rubbish burnt, become unbearable without BA. In fact, it was bloody lethal, apart from the one exception: Bert!

'Your uncle Bert's going to show you the intricacies of a Mark 4 Siebe Gorman Proto BA set.'

We toiled with the legion of lectures over the next few weeks. We were taught to dismantle the set completely down to the smallest segment, reassemble it, 'and make sure it's one hundred per cent, because your bloody life depends on it,' as Bert threatened. We had to learn parrot fashion the flow of oxygen through the sintered metal filters into the bag, through the cooler, into the inhaling tube, back into the exhaling tube, into the rear of the bag, through the carbon dioxide absorbent and back to the front of the bag to join the new supply of oxygen from the reducing valve. There, that was pretty easy – you all understood that, didn't you?

The set could be used in an emergency for up to eight hours, but would normally only last about an hour, unlike the short-duration compressed air sets. Having taken in the theory side we were now to be put to the test in the chamber. We stood outside apprehensively, our sets donned and started, ready to enter the inferno Bert was busily preparing for us below.

The steel doors burst open and thick billows of grey-black smoke belched upwards from the bowels of the pit, followed by a sub-officer with a deeply self-satisfied smirk on his countenance which would have passed as a fair impression of Al Jolson. The trainees stepped back as one, from the intense heat now being emitted from the chamber.

'Don't be shy, it's only a few old mattresses and oily rags. In you go now.'

I'd seen Tom and Jerry many times as a kid, and the smile on Bert's face was definitely that of the cat. I just hoped that we (the mice) would emerge triumphant from our trial.

As the team leader, Dave entered first and duly fell headlong down the stone steps, crashing into a pile of old burning dustbins that had been strategically placed across our designated route.

'Christ, that's only the first obstacle and that silly sod's found it already.' We could hear Bert bragging about his devious course from up above.

'You all right, Woodsie?'

'I'm okay, just banged my knee a bit, that's all Jim.'

The slamming of the heavy steel doors as they were closed echoed throughout the hollow chamber. I checked my CEAG lamp to make sure it was on. Unbelievably, it was!

'Christ, it's bloody dark down here,' said Ken Smith.

'I can't see sod all through these goggles; they're steamed up already,' I replied.

'That's it! Keep talking, O'Halloran, you'll choke to bleeding death if you don't shut up. That mouthpiece is supposed to be a seal.'

I couldn't believe it! Bert was down here with us and with no set. Vic was right; the man was bloody mental.

The heat was becoming unbearable as the exposed parts of my face started to scorch. The exertion of dragging a fully charged line of two and three quarter inch hose was also beginning to take its toll. We edged our way slowly forwards towards the distant red glow that appeared intermittently through the barrier of black smoke. We followed close to the walls, feeling in front of us using a sweeping movement with the backs of our hands. Our progress was slow and ponderous, as each step forward had to be checked to feel if any obstacles were on the floor, transferring the weight from the back foot to the front as we moved along.

We reached the pile of burning mattresses and opened the hand-controlled branch. The instant reaction of the water on the fire caused a terrifying gush of scalding hot steam to surge towards us, making the already intolerable conditions even more unbearable, but how could we possibly turn back in defeat when some silly sod was proving that he didn't even require a set.

We put out the fire, dragged ourselves and the hose up the Jacob's ladder at the rear of the chamber and emerged into the field, where we were welcomed back into the sunlight by Bert and Vic, who had been designated as BA controller.

'That wasn't too bad, was it? Now don't forget to ease your nose clips off very gently by prizing the spring clip apart like this.' He demonstrated the manoeuvre by easing Ken's clip apart between his index finger and thumb and delicately removing it from his nose. Now he moved over and stood next to me.

'Don't under any circumstances snatch it off like this.'

'Jesus Christ!' I yelled through my mouthpiece as half of the welded skin from my nose departed along with my nose clip. I grabbed my nose in the feverish belief that my hand would ease the pain but discovered that this only made it worse. Lifting one foot off the floor at a time and imitating a Sioux war dance didn't help much either. 'Fuck you Bert!' I continued my dance over to the ablutions where I poured copious quantities of cold water on to my glowing nose.

Over the remaining period of our BA training, we were taught the various intricacies of entrapped procedure, search procedure, the different stages of BA control and, once again, the necessity to become reliant not only on yourself but also on the team.

Stratford station was now being prepared for the grand opening and all three stations became involved in the drill displays we were to put on for the VIPs. We had been practising a pump escape and pump drill in collaboration with the other watches and I had struck up a friendship with Gordon Bliss, a stocky bloke with dark wavy hair, about six years my senior. Gordon lived in East Ham, just around the corner from us, and his wife Kay immediately hit it off with Joan. Our wives were not unlike in many ways; they were both extroverts, both outspoken and to say that these two ladies together were formidable was not an exaggeration.

The big day arrived on the 9th May, 1964, and the station was to be officially opened by Her Majesty's Inspector of Fire Services, Mr Charteris, along with the Lady Mayoress of West Ham and a Russian delegation. The interpreter for the Russians turned out to be my Jewish barber, Morry, from Forest Lane. It was quiet a culture shock to discover that Morry had other talents apart from the razor and flogging johnnies to the local teds.

The firemen who were taking part in the display were allowed to invite their wives. The drills went with the precision one would expect given the number of weeks we had been practising, and were greeted with rapturous applause by the spectators, especially Joan and Kay.

Unfortunately, the arrangements for taking tea and sandwiches by the invited guests afterwards were not as well planned. The dignitaries, officers and their wives were shown to their respective seats on the decorated balcony whilst firemen and their 'women' were seated out of sight around by the dustbins. It also transpired that the VIPs were partaking of wine, canapés, and finger sandwiches, whilst Joan and Kay had tea in a paper cup with doorstep sandwiches.

Gordon and I were sweating profusely from our efforts and were probably too exhausted to realise the ramifications of our responses to the girls' questions.

'Which one's the chief officer?' enquired Joan.

'The bloke on the balcony, with all the "salad cream" on the peak of his cap.'

'Right!' said Kay as they both marched off towards the balcony.

Gordon grimaced. 'Oh Christ, no, they're making a bee line for Chopper!' We stood there, mouths open, as they proceeded to verbally assault Mr Cutting.

'Oh my God, what in the name of Christ are they saying to him?' Gordon didn't answer but shook his head in total disbelief.

To our astonishment, the chief, a tall grey-haired distin-guished-looking gentleman, was listening intently, occasionally glancing over the balcony to confirm which two firemen the ladies were talking about. He then shook their hands and gesticulated for them to sit down beside the distinguished guests.

'We are in deep shit, Hooligan, deep, deep, shit!'

I didn't bother to answer, I just carried on drinking, thinking to myself that this was probably the last cup of tea I would ever have in the fire service.

'What the bloody hell did you say to him?' asked Gordon as the girls descended the stairs on their return.

'We just explained that we are as good as anyone else here and saw no reason to be stuck by the dustbins like trash,' replied Joan.

'He's a really nice man,' Kay went on. 'He agreed with us and even wanted to know who we were married to.'

'I bet he fucking well did,' uttered Gordon like a man condemned to the dole queue.

The following morning at 9 a.m., Sub-Officer Cross was taking the roll call. The chief officer had just told the duty man that he was mobile to headquarters and was walking past the parade to his car. Cross stopped calling the roll to allow Mr Cutting to pass.

'Morning, sir.'

'Morning, Sub, carry on.' He took another three steps, then stopped dead and turned slowly round. I was trying to step discreetly back in the vain hope that the large frame of Paul Janes, our union rep, would obscure me.

'Ah yes! Fireman O'Halloran,' he said thoughtfully, 'and tell me, how are your good lady wife and that of Fireman Bliss this morning? Well, I hope.'

I coughed to clear my drying throat. 'Very well, thank you, sir.'

He nodded and looked up towards the ceiling as if he were trying to imprint a mental note on to it: 'Get this bugger later!' He slammed the door of his Corsair shut and drove out of the yard.

Being a small brigade we tried to cope with the limited resources we had, but on occasions we had to request the assistance of the outer brigades, like Essex, East Ham and London. They were only called upon as a last desperate measure. London's crews would only attend an incident for a maximum of three hours before they were relieved; they were able to do this because of the huge number of personnel they had available over the capital. At a protracted incident it was not uncommon for us in West Ham to work twelve hours before being relieved, especially if we had a hoof and horn ship alight in the docks.

These ships, bound for the cattle-feed mills in the Victoria Dock, would catch light at sea. The cargo holds would be covered and carbon dioxide pumped into them until they reached the dock. Once the hatches were released the new intake of oxygen would ignite the cargo once more, and that's when we would be called. Because of the extended times we would spend on such incidents, we were probably far more experienced firemen than those in other brigades. We spent a lot of time on topography; you were expected to know every street or road in the brigade, along with knowledge of the Royal Docks, in particular the gate numbers and the hours that the gates would be open. Ship fires were our bread and butter in West Ham.

Brian Chillcott, who trained with me at Southwark, had a really gruesome job on one of the ships. It was a small fire in a crew members' cabin. A severely burnt body had been discovered in this cabin. As they lifted the body, the extreme charring made it break in two. Whether or not this affected him, Brian left the brigade soon afterwards.

On occasions we were ordered to stand by for the watch at another station, for various reasons: sickness, annual leave and so on. I was ordered to stand by at Silvertown for the night shift. I packed my kit bag with my fire gear and drove down to Canning Town. It was easier that way because the bascule and swing bridges across the docks could be avoided. If a ship was entering the docks you could be stuck for hours when a bridge was up.

Silvertown Fire Station was in desperate need of renovation, but due to the imminent 'takeover' by London these needs were put on hold. The main building, which faced south on to North Woolwich Road, was a single-storey brick-built, four-bayed structure which housed the fire engines, offices and sleeping quarters. A separate 'building' (for want of a better adjective) stood (and I use that word reservedly) on the west side of the drill yard behind the main complex. This was used as a recreation area and mess room. It was heated by means of a cast-iron coal 'range' that would not have been out of place in a John Wayne western. It terminated through a corrugated tin roof by way of an eight foot cast-iron pipe. You could even brew up on the stove's hot plate. The toilet, of course, was of the 'al fresco' variety.

I reported my arrival to Station Officer, McGinty, another second-generation Irishman, famed within the job for numerous run-ins with the establishment. After supper I sat round the glowing stove with the watch, waiting for the kettle to brew.

'Cuppa, Jim?' asked the mess man.

I was sorely tempted to drawl, 'The hell I will.'

'No thanks, Terry,' I replied. He was about to pass the cup to McGinty, when the bells went down.

'King George 5th, 12 shed,' shouted the watch room man. 'Boat on fire.'

'I've told you before,' remonstrated McGinty, 'they're bloody ships, not boats.'

We turned left out of the station along North Woolwich Road, over the Silvertown bypass and into number 19 gate.

'Look at that bugger go,' shouted the driver as we sped along the south side of the King George 5th dock. Flames had engulfed the entire deck of the ship. McGinty began to ring the bell vigorously, to convey to the scurrying people on deck that we had arrived.

'Slip the escape up to the front of the ship,' shouted McGinty. 'Get some sets on quick.' The Escapes crew frantically pulled the fifty foot wheeled ladder off the machine and began extending it, simultaneously wheeling it to the side of the ship.

The pump's crew took rolled lengths of hose up the swaying gangplank on to the deck ready for an all-out assault on the inferno.

'For Christ's sake, who called you?' screamed a guy in a long leather coat. 'I don't bloody well believe it.' He began waving his arms about hysterically and stamping his foot on the deck. 'Hold it, hold everything, darlings,' he instructed to the people behind him.

The smoke and flames quickly dispersed as the gas jets and smoke machines on the deck were switched off. The gay guy pinched McGinty's face and shook his cheek forcefully.

'You have just ruined four hours' work in setting up.' As each word was forced out, he tugged synchronistically at Paddy's cheek. 'You have just destroyed my bloody film.' Paddy's mouth was gaping wider with the increasing attack on his face.

'Nobody bothered to tell us, mate,' retorted McGinty as his face was released from the vice-like grip. 'Either you or the PLA should have told us, then we wouldn't have had this balls-up, would we?' He started to rub his reddening face. 'And another bloody thing, *darling*, if you ever grab me like that again, your balls will end up under your sodding chin.' Paddy had never quite grasped the finer points of the brigade etiquette when dealing with members of the public.

We hurriedly made up our gear and started to drive back to the station. On reaching the dock gate, a PLA police officer waved us down.

'Sorry, lads, you were given the wrong shed. It's round the other side, some rubbish on the quayside.'

The fire engines turned around as McGinty put the flashing blue lights on and began ringing the bells with a demonic relish as we rushed past the film crew. The director, I swear, was ready to launch himself off the deck into the dock as Paddy wound his window down and blew him a lingering kiss.

I have seen many adventure films since, but, surprisingly, never recognised that scene in any of them.

My initiation into the 'glamour' of wearing BA for the first time came on my return to Plaistow for the following shift. Stratford were already attending an incident and we were ordered on to their ground at Dames Road, Forest Gate. We were greeted upon our arrival by an excited neighbour who told Silvers that an old lady lived in the house and that he thought she was still in there. Daisy set-up the stage one BA board as Bert, Jeff, Vic and myself struggled into our sets.

'Me and Vic will do downstairs,' said Bert. 'You two search the first floor.' The rest of the crews ran out hose from the street hydrant to the pump and slipped the thirty-five foot extension ladder to the first floor window as an alternative means of escape if the internal stairs went. Silvers climbed back into the cab and grabbed the radio. 'From Station Officer Silvers, make fumps pour,' he shouted excitedly.

'I see the guv's got his new teeth in,' quipped Vic as we prepared to enter the house. Silvers was frantically fishing around in his mouth to adjust his teeth.

'Fucking things,' he went on. 'From Station Officer Silvers, make pumps four, persons reported.'

He successfully got the message across just as the offending dentures slithered out on to the dashboard.

By now the blackened windows were beginning to crack.

'Put a spray jet on to those windows,' shouted Silvers, pointing to the net curtains as they burst into flames from the cocktail of heat and fresh air. We dragged the hose-reel up the stairs and on to the landing, feeling gingerly with our feet for any burnt floorboards.

Jeff mumbled something and pointed towards the back room and then to himself. He then signalled for me to search the front room. I passed through the open door and edged along by the parting wall. Once again I couldn't see a bloody thing due to the smoke and the goggles misting up. This must be the airing cupboard, I thought, as I reached the corner of the room and opened a door. A pile of something cascaded down on top of me. I groped around, picked up a bundle and drew it up towards my lamp. Clothes and newspapers! I felt tentatively behind the door, imagining a body there but deep down hoping not to make the discovery. I put a hand into the cupboard, very, very slowly. Feels sticky: must be something that's melted. I continued around the room, keeping close to the wall and passing the window, which afforded more light now that the net curtain had been torn down by the force of water from the jet at street level. Smoke billowed from the window as I poked my head out and gave Woodsie the thumbs up. So far so good. I stumbled over a chair as I made my way diagonally across the centre of the room and fell on to the bed. Jesus! I hope she's not in it. My arm stretched warily across the bed. Christ! What's that? Cats – they said she kept cats. The animal was obviously dead. I crawled back and placed it underneath the window. I made my way back on to the double bed. Well she's not in there, thank God.

'How's it going, Hooly?' Jeff had entered the room.

'Just checking under the bed now,' I mumbled through my mouthpiece.

'Nothing in the back,' said Jeff.

I completed the search, then we made our way downstairs, passing Bert and Vic in the hall.

'We're just going to check the basement,' muttered Bert. We raised our thumbs in acknowledgement and made our way out into the bright daylight.

Daisy started to grimace as I tried to collect my tally from him. He's not going to faint again, I thought. I knew Jeff had cut his hand on some glass but it wasn't that bad. Jeff looked at me quizzically, as we were both getting the same reaction from Daisy. Both he and Bob Annis were backing off as we tried to approach them. 'What's up?' I yanked my mouthpiece out and lifted my goggles on to my forehead. It wasn't until I removed the nose clip that the unmistakable smell of cat shit wafted up from my tunic into my nostrils.

I turned towards Jeff. We were both covered in it!

'For Christ's sake, hose 'em down, Woods,' spluttered Silvers, the absence of his teeth making his mouth even more lopsided. Woodsie's face was losing its colour and fast approaching that ashen hue it had when he was about to throw up.

'I think he's going to puke,' said Jeff.

Daisy dropped the hose and rushed to the rear of the appliance.

'Not again,' said Silvers. 'Smiffy, wash them down and get Woods to clear his mess up as well.'

Dave was holding his stomach and slowly regaining his composure when Bert and Vic emerged in the same sorry state as us. Dave grabbed the handrail of the pump for support and started to heave once more.

'Oh for Christ's sake, Woodsie, you should be used to a bit of shit by now after the sewage works,' moaned Bert.

The seat of the fire had been discovered by Vic and Bert on the ground floor. The smoke was clearing quickly as Silvers passed McGinty on his way into the house.

Paddy was coughing hoarsely as he sat on a dustbin and pulled a Woodbine out of his tobacco pouch. He shut his eyes in ecstasy as he drew a deep breath into his already smoke-filled lungs.

'Christ, I needed that.' He took another deep breath. 'The whole place is covered in cat shit and piss – you two must have been rolling in it.' He chuckled contentedly. 'Glad we got here after you – saved my lads getting covered in it.' By now his amusement could hardly be contained as he watched us disrobe behind the salvage sheet being held up to protect the public from the striptease act being performed by Bert.

'Where's the old girl, then?' asked Ken Smith.

'She turned up about ten minutes ago. Been shopping,' said one of Silvertown's crew. 'They reckon she's got over forty cats in there. They never go out.'

'Paddy, see if you can get the council down to sort this out. I'm taking this lot back to Plaistow to clean up.' Silvers ushered us towards our engines from a respectable distance. The red carbolic was much in evidence on our return as we scrubbed ourselves almost red to try to get the acrid smell off our bodies. Vic pulled the curtain aside, wolf-whistled and duly emptied the freezing cold contents of a bucket of water over me.

'Bastard,' I yelled as a broad grin spread across his battered countenance. At some time, he had been a professional boxer – not a very good one by the state of his face and by his own admission. He said that he had been knocked out so many times that he had had 'Vic Evans,

Builder and Decorator' painted on the soles of his boxing boots.

At first, like many others, I had the misconstrued idea that he was a bit punch-drunk, but quickly realised that he had a very sharp brain and a wicked self-mocking sense of humour. Jeff and Vic had been at Plaistow together for about three years before I arrived, but I quickly found that I had more in common with them than with any of the others on the watch and a deep friendship evolved between us.

*

'Poor old Woodsie threw another wobbler, then.' Alan Cobb, one of the turntable operators who hadn't attended the incident, had obviously been told of Dave's predicament.

'Yeah, it's taking a long time, but he'll get used to it eventually,' replied Vic as we went into the recreation room.

Alan sat himself down in one of the armchairs as Dave entered the room.

'Fancy a game, Jim?' said Vic, taking a snooker cue from the rack.

'As long as the old man doesn't see me – he reckons I should be studying the manuals like Dave there.'

Dave smiled and sat down beside Alan, pulling the manual on building construction from his case.

'Are you taking the Leading Fireman's written exam, Jim?' he inquired.

'I've put in for it, Dave, but I don't think I stand a chance in hell; I haven't studied enough. Still, you never know.'

'How about you, Vic?'

'You must be joking, Daisy. I used my allocation of brains up just trying to get into this bleeding job.'

'And you, Jeff?'

'No way, Dave, couldn't stand all the aggravation of being an officer. I'm quite happy as I am, mate.'

Jeff's answer could have applied to the best part of the watch. A pity, really, because some of them certainly had the academic ability, and someone like Alan Cobb would have made a good junior officer. He was a thin, wiry-looking man, in his early forties, and reminded me in looks of Trevor Howard. He was a great reader and an excellent photographer, but could be contrary, like the time he was showing us some of his colour slides of nude models. Alan was trying to educate us in the finer points of his art, but as soon as the ribald comments started, he turned off the projector, snatched his slides up and stormed out of the room. His ability with the TL was honed to the same sense of perfection and pride. He never ceased to amaze me. Even under the most stressful of conditions, he could pull up at a job and assess the height and inclination required to pitch the hundred foot ladder within an inch of a designated spot. It was his incredible ability that motivated me to dream of becoming a TL operator one day, but that was a long way off. I had first to become a heavy goods driver.

Chapter Six

'Come on, pay up or you'll get no grub next week.' Bob Annis slid the mess tin along the table. Our twelve shillings and sixpence would enable Bob to provide us with two lunches and sandwiches on days and two breakfasts and two dinners on nights. He would do the shopping in his off-duty period and be responsible for the cooking along with a mess assistant. Surprisingly, most of the guys were good cooks. Unfortunately, I did not fall into that category. I had become infamous for my lumpy porridge and crispy fried eggs.

'O'Halloran ought to pay more than us,' moaned Bert. 'He sods everything up.'

'As long as he can make runny custard, he's okay,' said Jeff with a wry smile.

I had found out that the watch deliberately made the custard very weak and runny in order to infuriate the 'guv'nor'. Because of his deformed mouth, the custard would run out the side and down his chin, much to his annoyance and the delight of the younger element of the watch, who were subjected to his tyrannical rule. He would delight in deliberately trapping someone if they had forgotten to place a watch or some article of clothing in their open locker. The article would be snatched up by him and hurriedly rushed to his office. He would then wait for the unfortunate loser to go cap in hand and report the article missing. A report would have to be completed by the fireman in which he would have to admit negligence on his part, which of course could lead to disciplinary proceedings, something which Silvers took a sneering, childish relish in emphasising. The charge was seldom put; the pleasure he got was the sense of power he had been able to use.

Jeff, Vic, Daisy, Smithy and myself were the obvious targets, as the older hands had learnt to deal with his idiosyncrasies. Vic seemed to get more abuse than most. He hated the old man and so spent most of his time devising schemes to get back at him. Once he wrapped an old piece of fish in newspaper, placed it in a shoebox and made a parcel with brown paper and ribbon. This was then placed on a chair in the rec room for the trap to be sprung. As expected, Silvers grabbed it with glee and rushed it to his office where he put it in his locker, awaiting the claimant who, of course, never materialised.

After about two weeks, the officer in charge of Red watch, Bert Bottomley, asked Silvers if he could smell anything weird in the station officer's office, as certain remarks had been made by different personnel about a strange odour in the room. They established that the smell was coming from Silvers's locker and duly unwrapped the offending parcel. The rotten fish by this time was way past its sell-by date and nearly walked out of the box with the aid of the maggots. Vic had triumphed, but Silvers didn't mention a word about the incident. He would bide his time, find out who the culprit was and exact his revenge later. After a few weeks, the story became folklore within the brigade and Victor had assumed the mantle of superhero. Sid Silvers now knew the culprit and planned the inevitable act of revenge.

This came about one night shift when Vic had the last watch between 5 a.m. and 7 a.m. Vic had signed on in the log book and started to doze off in the chair. Silvers had kept himself awake in order to catch Vic out in some way and couldn't believe his luck when he saw Vic asleep through the window in the door. He gently turned the handle and sidled up to the desk. The only light in the room, a small table lamp, shone directly on to the log book. Silvers could hardly contain himself. The log was an official legal document and could be used in a court of law. The loss of such a book would inevitably lead to a charge with a punishment of loss of wages or even dismissal. A reduction in rank could not apply as Vic was already on the bottom rung. If Silvers could have turned cartwheels, he would have. He gently lifted the book off the table, crept silently out and scurried across the appliance bay in his stockinged feet, back to his bed in his office.

Vic woke me at 7.10 a.m. for my watch.

'You're late, Vic,' I said, rubbing my eyes, as I entered the watch room.

'Yeah, I had to wait until that sneaky little bastard went to sleep.' He nodded towards the office. 'He came over here and thought I was asleep, so he nicked the log and took it over to his office.'

'So where is it now?'

'On the sodding boiler. I got it back while he was asleep.'

My mouth dropped open. 'You're joking!' I said, waiting for Vic to produce the book from behind his back. He shook his head as a huge smile spread across his face.

'Christ, you're *not* joking, he'll go bloody spare! He'll throw the book at you.'

'What bloody book? He was the last one with it.'

'Christ, here he comes.' I began to panic.

'What's the matter, old O'Halloran? You look worried.' The words slithered from the corner of his mouth.

'Er, er I was—'

'It's all right, Guv, I was just explaining to Jim that you came over during the night and took the log book. I suppose you were checking something, but we had better have it back now, Guv, if you don't mind – we've got a few bookings to do!' Silvers's face was a picture of total confusion and bewilderment, and after dashing back over to his office and frantically searching for the book, only confirmed to the two 'witnesses' (Vic and myself) that he was the last person to have the log book in his possession.

'What's the matter, Guv, can't you find it?' enquired Vic.

Papers were being strewn across the room as Silvers frenziedly sought the log.

'Didn't put it in your locker, Guv, did you?' I asked.

'No, no. I definitely put it on my desk.' He hesitated. 'Or maybe on the chair.'

Vic went through the motions of concern by lifting a few papers.

'No, it's definitely not here, Guv.'

'Anyway, old Evans, you were asleep in the watch room.' Silvers tried to go on the offensive.

'I couldn't have been, Guv, or how would I know you took it?'

Silvers obviously wanted to say something but his brain had blanked for a few seconds.

'You're in on this, old O'Halloran,' he blurted.

'Me, Guv? I've only just got up.'

Silvers started to pull his locker to pieces like a demented being.

'Get back in the bloody watch room,' he screamed at us.

Vic winked at me and we left, gently closing the door, as the heavier gear in Silvers's locker cluttered to the floor. 'Bastards, I'll have the bastards.' The words were spat out with venom.

'Don't say a word to anyone about this, Jim, let's see how the little bugger gets out of this one.' A huge self-satisfied grin spread over Vic's craggy features.

In fact the 'little bugger' did manage to slither his way out of it. We had a shout almost immediately and upon our return Silvers informed the watch that the log book and 'some other' items had gone missing from his office. He even had the front to say that if it was one of our pranks, he wouldn't take any disciplinary action as long as the log book was replaced. It was eventually recorded that the book had been stolen by persons unknown.

Silvers's ability as a fireman was unquestionable but his attitude towards his staff, particularly the younger members, was one of constant antagonism. It appeared that he had to constantly prove to himself and the watch that he was the 'guv'nor'. Maybe it had something to do with his lack of inches or possibly his deformity.

'How did his mouth and neck get like that, Jeff – a fire was it?'

'No, no one really knows, Jim. The story goes that he fell asleep with a cigarette in the corner of his mouth and when he woke up it was stuck to his lip.'

'Yeah, but then the silly sod kept picking the scab,' interrupted Bert, 'until it got so bad that he had to have a skin graft from his neck.'

'I don't believe it,' said Daisy.

'Well, that's the story we heard,' said Jeff, 'and nobody's contradicted it yet.'

'That's probably why he uses a cigarette holder now,' said Vic, trying to confirm the rumour, 'but that didn't make him into an evil little git – he was born like that.'

Whilst most of us disliked Silvers and were aware of the power he held over us, as far as our jobs were concerned, Vic seemed to take it upon himself not only to get retribution for himself but for those on the watch who were unwilling to stand up to him. It turned into a battle of wits between Silvers and the watch with neither side willing to admit to being beaten, even under the most harassing conditions.

Bob Annis collected the rest of the mess money and made his entries in the book.

'That's left me skint!'

'Haven't you got any part time, Jim?' enquired Vic.

'I do a bit of window cleaning with my father-in-law, but the bloody rain hasn't helped over the last few weeks.'

'Put your name down for the security run on Fridays.'

'What's that?'

'Chopper has arranged with the council a nice little part-time job for us. We have to go round with the wages van to all the council schools, hospitals and depots and just guard the clerk while he's giving out the wages.'

'You have to wear your undress uniform, though,' said Bert.

Most of the watch did a bit of moonlighting. In fact, some of them were excellent tradesmen: electricians, plumbers, decorators and car mechanics, and although the brigade frowned upon it, there was nothing they could do to stop it when we were off duty. Even the hard-line trade unionists among us seemed to let their principle, of one man, one job drop if it meant a few bob, cash in hand.

The security job was only available when we were off duty, and because the run took place on Fridays only, the earning capability was somewhat restricted due to our duty system. The 'diamonds' gave me and Percy a little extra but could be erratic because of inclement weather, and so I put my name forward for the security job. Payment was taxable and shown as overtime on our payslips. Even with the little extras our pay, considering the nature and unsocial hours was still well below that of other industries, but the job satisfaction I got far outweighed the minuses. At least when we turned up people were generally pleased to see us and the job gave Joan and myself a secure base for our life together.

The brigade covered a diversity of risks, ranging from flour mills, chemical factories, sugar refineries, the docks and a large railway complex, both underground and mainline. The majority of railway incidents we attended were, unfortunately, of the kind we picked up on our next tour of duty.

'Person fallen under train, West Ham station.' Silvers clipped the call slip on to the dash. The emergency tender and pump escape followed us out of the station and down towards the A13. The traffic lights at the junction with Manor Road were red. Alan Cobb double-declutched the gearbox of the Merryweather from third to second as we swung on to the wrong side of the road to avoid the confused cars and lorries we were bearing down on. The ET and PE were clanging their bells in impatient unison as they tucked in behind the pump.

Silvers started to increase the momentum of his hand movement on the leather strap as we passed the old Memorial ground. The original home of West Ham FC, then known as the Thames Ironworks. Vic mockingly blessed himself, as anything to do with the Hammers was held tantamount to the Holy Grail.

I grabbed the first aid kit from the back shelf and continued to try to do the buttons up on my tunic as the pump swayed alarmingly from side to side. The ambulance, which had been called at the same time as ourselves, approached the station from the opposite direction and screeched to halt outside the booking hall as we pulled up. All four doors of the pump burst open in unison as we scrambled on to the pavement.

'Give them a hand to get the heavy lifting gear off the ET,' shouted Bert to the PE crew. They manhandled the seven-ton wheeled jack off the ET and carried it down the wooden stairs, their leather boots clattering in unison as the rate of decent increased. The driver of the train was being attended to by railway staff and gently persuaded by the police to go with them upstairs. He was an elderly man in his late fifties, frail and obviously in shock. The transport staff were busy trying to clear the platforms of those members of the public who seemed indignant that they were not going to get a ringside seat for the performance.

'If you don't move, sir, I'll nick you,' threatened a policeman to one of the more obstinate passengers, who was remonstrating that he had bought a ticket and had every right to be there. The constable grabbed his arm, pushed it behind his back and frogmarched the idiot towards the stairs.

Ken Smith had grabbed two railway horns off the pump escape and put one of the reflective jackets on, along with Bob. They made their way to either end of the station and took up their position as lookouts, to avoid further danger to the crews.

'He's under the front bogie of the second carriage, apparently just dived in front of it, poor sod,' said one of the staff.

We lowered the jack down on to the permanent way, taking it in front of the train and around to the opposite side, away from the platform, so that we had more room to manoeuvre the gear.

'The front carriage has been uncoupled,' shouted the railwayman. 'We'll move it along for you.' We knelt down beside the front end of the second carriage and peered underneath.

'Oh Christ!' Daisy burbled, turning his usual ashen grey as he gazed down at the remains of the body beneath the train.

'You'd better go back, Dave,' I said sympathetically.

'Oh no he don't, he's going to bloody well stay here with me,' said Bert grabbing Daisy by the sleeve. 'I'll make you into a bleeding fireman if it kills me.'

Vic pulled my arm away from Dave and nodded his approval of Bert's assessment.

'It's just a job now, Dave, the poor bugger's dead anyway. Got to get used to it, son,' said Jeff.

We gently jacked the carriage up, inch by inch, until we had enough room to block it up, making the area underneath safe to work in.

'What do you need, Bert?' enquired Silvers.

'Not a lot, Guv, just a salvage sheet and some bags of sand to soak up,' replied Bert. 'Oh and a couple of shovels. Ask the law to get a box from the mortuary – the ambulance blokes won't take this little lot.'

We could now see that the victim had initially fallen on his back with his head pointing towards the oncoming train. The suction, caused by the train, had pulled his shirt from his body and lifted him up under the carriage and into the wheels, taking both his legs off above the knees. The lower part of his abdomen had been ripped open from his genitals to just below his rib cage. Part of his scrotum was lying near his neck. There was a reluctance from any of the crew to start picking the pieces up to put into the sheet. It had gone deathly quiet.

'Fucking worse case of mumps I've ever seen.'

We turned towards Bert in disbelief at first, and then, incredibly, smiles began to cross our faces, as we realised that he had brought us back to the task in hand and had taken the reality and horror out of the situation with his incredible remark.

'You rotten bastard,' said Daisy.

'Yeah, but you're smiling, son,' replied Bert, intimating that Dave had at long last cracked it.

He put his arm around Dave's shoulder and pulled him affectionately towards him.

'Watch him Dave, I think he fancies you,' said Vic, laughingly.

We collected the remains of the body up and placed it into the salvage sheet, to wait for the police surgeon to pronounce that the poor guy was officially dead. Bert had taken some papers out of the trouser pocket and handed them to the police.

'Okay, Guv, we'll go back with the ET and PE. The pump's crew can put it into the box when it comes,' he said, pointing towards the bloodstained sheet. We arrived back at the station to be greeted by a police sergeant who informed us that the guy who jumped was a patient at Goodmayes Hospital and was being treated for previous attempted suicides.

'Poor bastard got it right this time,' said Vic philosophically. 'Jesus, you must be in some state of mind to do that.' He shook his head in a slow, remorseful manner.

I arrived home that evening and after dinner sat myself in front of the coal fire ready to read the *Daily Mirror*.

'The Beatles are on *Top of the Pops* tonight. Don't know whether I like them or not,' said Joan. 'It's funny, because Mum and Dad like them.'

'I'm surprised your dad likes them, with that long hair.'

'Well, at least they're not going thin on top like you, I only married you for your curly hair,' she bent over and playfully kissed the top of my head. I leapt out of the chair and grabbed Joan by the waist as she screamed, trying to avoid me. We tumbled to the floor and I grabbed both her arms, pining her beneath me.

'And I only married you, because you've got lovely big tits.' I leant forward and kissed each breast.

'Stop sodding about, you'll wake Corinne up.'

I pulled Joan up off the floor and embraced her.

'Oh, there's a letter on the shelf for you, looks official.'

I opened it tentatively and started to read.

'What's the matter, what's it say?'

'Jesus, I've only passed the Leading Fireman's written.'

'Never thought you wouldn't, big 'ead.' Joan kissed me tenderly as she took the letter to read.

The day had been a typical 'fire brigade' day, low one minute, high the next. In a short space of time I had seen tragedies the ordinary person would only see once in a lifetime and had experienced the elation of successfully rescuing some poor bugger from a crash or fire. I had enjoyed the warmth and camaraderie of a group of guys who were unique in their dedication to the service and finally was able to go home to a wife who made me feel ten feet tall. She must have worried herself sick sometimes, wondering if I'd come home and if she would manage if something happened. She always told her friends proudly, 'It takes a special kind of bloke to be a fireman.'

For me, it took an exceptional woman to be a fireman's wife.

Chapter Seven

The small family compactness of the West Ham Brigade was due to be shattered in the very near future as the rumours that had been circulating were now being translated into reality. The watch room at Stratford was being refurbished with a new consul that would be responsible for thirty stations or the new Eastern Command as it was to be known. Promotions were being strewn about like confetti, especially the positions above station officer rank as these didn't require academic qualifications. They just needed the nod from the right person. It was even suggested that one particular officer was interviewed by the fire brigade committee and asked by the chairman to 'tell us a bit about yourself', which seemed somewhat ridiculous as the chairman happened to be the father-in-law of the officer.

My personal promotion was still some way off as I had yet to pass the Leading Fireman's practical exam and then the interview. The idea of being 'lost' in a large brigade was abhorrent to us; we felt that our individuality, pride and not to mention the extra ten bob we received each week over and above the other brigades would be devoured by this colossus. It would be top-heavy and have so many personnel they'd be able to trample the bloody fires out.

Anyway, we got lost the other side of Bow Bridge!

'Heard about the new set-up?' asked Don Igglesden, one of Silvertown's crew, as we pulled up besides their engines at the Royal Victoria Dock.

'You'll be retired before they take over, mate,' replied Bert.

We had been called to a hoof and horn ship alight alongside the CWS mills. The ship's cargo had caught fire at sea. Before we could attack the fire, lengthy and complicated negotiations had to take place between the dockers' union, the ship's owners and the PLA to come to a rate for unloading the dangerous cargo. The unions always appeared to win, as their main gambit was, 'Well, if you don't pay that, the fucking boat can burn,' which of course brought the bargaining to a quick conclusion.

The dockers at this time were much like ourselves, as rumours were rife that the Royal Docks were going to close and job losses would be imminent in the next few years; therefore, I had a certain sympathy for their hardline attitudes, which some people described as greed. At least I wasn't about to lose my job.

Station Officer McGinty led our crew on to the ship, whilst the 'negotiations' continued on the dockside. Two crews below were setting up hydrants and hose lines in preparation for the eventual attack.

'Bring some BA sets up here,' Paddy shouted down to Stratford's crew.

'They're all bleeding chinks on this ship,' he muttered to us as we made our way along the deck. 'You speakee English?' he enquired of one puzzled-looking deck hand. 'Jesus, it's bloody hopeless,' he went on as we passed the vacant stare from another crew member.

'I heard someone say the officers were Spanish, if that's any help,' I said.

'Same fuckin' fing, ain't it, they're bleedin' foreigners.'

Jeff pointed towards the bridge. 'That's the captain up there, Guv.'

'Right, leave this to me lads. I've been to Spain on 'oliday.'

We followed our leader, totally dumbfounded but in some awe at Paddy's shock disclosure of his linguistic abilities. Our esteem had shot off the Richter scale. McGinty pulled his squat frame up the stairs leading to the bridge with us in hot pursuit, ready to witness this bilingual revelation.

The captain opened the door and met us outside. He was a tall, elegant-looking man. He peered over his glasses and looked down at McGinty.

'Mio officerio in chargeo firemen.' There was silence from us as McGinty pointed in our direction. Maybe the bloody ship would sink, I thought to myself, as the full realisation of Paddy's linguistic talents became embarrassingly clear.

'We puto fire outo, when covers off.' The Spaniard looked quizzically at McGinty's pugnacious face.

'I don't fink he understands,' said McGinty, turning towards us, obviously surprised at the lack of comprehension the Spaniard had for his mother tongue. Vic and Jeff were trying to slowly edge their way off the bridge. The embarrassment was becoming too much.

'Oi, where do you two fink you're going. I 'aven't finished wiv this bloke yet.' Their faces took on a blank, moronic expression as Paddy continued to display his prowess not only with the language but also with the addition of sign language. 'He still can't understand a bloody fing.' McGinty was now in a perplexed state.

'Exactly what is it you require, Station Officer?'

McGinty looked totally shell-shocked as the question was put to him in perfect BBC English. His mouth twisted into a formation ready to erupt into a language far removed from Spanish or English, but was restrained by the strangled laughter and broad grins as his face met ours.

'If you three tarts are just going to stand there pissing yourselves, you can go and help the others. Give these three wankers somefing to do, Bert,' McGinty shouted down.

The hatches were taken off once we had laid the hose lines out, and those who were to be closest to the fire had already donned their BA sets. Billows of foul-smelling smoke rose from the ship's hold and wafted over the dockside cranes and warehouses as the jets of water cascaded into the bowels of the ship. The grey cloud expanded itself with each drift until it seemed that the whole Canning Town skyline was enveloped in the cancerous mass.

'Make sure you keep track of the BA crews, Sid.' McGinty pointed towards the figures leaning over the hold, as they intermittently became visible through the smoke. The hoof and horn, which was ground at the mill for fertiliser and animal feed, had to be systematically pulled apart by crews working in the hold using hooks, shovels and forks, and then dampened down before the cranes could wrench it from the hold and transfer it to the dockside to be doused down again with spray jets, loaded on to lorries and dumped.

The heat in the hold was by now unbearable and the foul odour from the amputated animal limbs was beginning to affect the crews without BA.

'We'll have to put the relief crew on deck upwind,' shouted Bert to Silvers. 'They're getting a right gutful down here.'

Stratford's crew were moved from the dockside on to the ship, ready to take over from Silvertown's lads.

'When Stratford's boys come out, we'll take over,' Silvers volunteered.

'What about supper?' queried Bob Annis.

'We don't need any supper, there's plenty of tea and sarnies in the crew's mess. We can stay here 'till the morning, no problem, old Annis.' The nasal twang evaporated into a sneering grin as we realised that Silvers wasn't joking.

'Fifteen bloody hours on this shitheap,' Vic retorted.

'What's the matter, old Evans, can't take it?'

'Fucking lunatic,' muttered Vic as he pulled the charged hose along the deck.

'You say something, Evans?'

'No, Guv.'

'What time do you want the relief, then, Guv?'

'7.30 will do nicely, Bert.'

'Are you sure, Sid?' asked Paddy McGinty. He could see that we were not relishing the idea of a shift that long.

'No problem,' Silvers repeated, knowing full well that none of the other officers would have committed their crews to such a stint and that this would confirm his status amongst the other crews as a real nasty bastard.

We worked solidly through the night in a sequence of one hour shifts, first in the hold, then on the dockside damping down. We were allowed three half-hour breaks during the fifteen hours, one of which was spent in the ship's mess in the auspicious company of Jack Dash, one of the leaders of the dockers' union.

Jack enthralled us with his vision of the ever-changing responsibilities of the unions with regard to members' needs. One remark he made was to be prophetic in years to come, when I was involved in the first ever fire service strike. We in London were not over-keen to 'walk out', but had made plans to stay in and work to rule and use other dubious methods to beat the government, which just happened to be Labour. We realised that we were a small union and without the support of our senior officers and in particular the airport fire service we were on a hiding to nothing. The Labour Party knew they had other industries and services lining up in the pay queue who had far more clout than us and therefore they were willing to take us on and beat us, with the help of the army, and make an example of us. Unfortunately, we were outvoted by the other regions on strike action and being a democratic body we were embroiled in the three-month winter strike of 1978. We eventually returned to work with no more money than was originally offered, but at least we had secured a pay formula, which every subsequent government wants to destroy.

If we had taken to heart the words of Jack Dash – that walking through the gates was finished as a tactic – we could have still secured the same result without the hardships we had to endure. It may have taken longer, but morale would have still been reasonably high and the animosity between the men and the officers would not have sunk to the despairing depths it reached after the strike.

We watched the daylight break over the bleak Silvertown skyline as the early shift crane operators made their way up the Jacob's ladders to their cabins to start unloading the other ships.

'Come on, let's go home,' said Bert as Silvertown's crew pulled up alongside number 4 berth.

'Christ, you lot look shagged out,' said Don Igglesden as he waited for us to get off the ship's ladder and into our waiting appliance.

'So would you be, if you had a scatty bastard like that in charge.' Bert nodded towards Silvers, who had a contented grin on his face as he climbed up into the cab. I tried to pull my tunic up over my ears as I rested my head against the wooden side panel of the pump, but the constant buffeting I got as we drove over the uneven road surface stopped any intentions I may have had of trying to close my eyes.

'I am absolutely knackered.'

Jeff grinned sympathetically towards me.

My arms and back ached so much through the constant shovelling that I began to wish I was back navvying for the railway. I certainly never worked that hard on the track.

We returned to the station, had breakfast and left the oncoming watch to clean the fire engines.

Don Igglesden had decided to hold his retirement party at Plaistow, as the facilities were better than those at his own station. The appliances had been removed from the bays and driven on to the forecourt. The on-duty watch had been preparing the rec room, to accommodate the buffet. We already had a built-in bar – 'The Long Branch', which was the responsibility of all three watches. It was well stocked and officially only used by off-duty personnel, but providing the lads were sensible, a blind eye was turned on the odd occasion to the one pint. The disco was set-up in the bay for the dancing, and bunting adorned the exposed roof trusses.

Most people turned up in casual gear, save for the one exception, Tom Delarue of Stratford White watch, a tall, well-built man with jet black wavy hair and of Latin appearance. Tom made a grand entrance that would have put Noel Coward to shame, in an elegant evening dress suit complete with red bow tie and carnation in his lapel. He brushed past the dancers, grabbed Mrs Igglesden's hand and gently kissed the back of it.

'Good old Tom, trust him to go completely over the bloody top.' Gordon Bliss was well used to the eccentricities of Mr Delarue.

'Wait till you come back to Stratford, Jim, you'll find out about our Tom.'

'Back to Stratford! What do you mean?'

'Haven't you heard? Some of you are pencilled in before the takeover in April.'

'That's six months away.'

'Yeah, but the moves are due long before that.'

I didn't really like the idea of going back to Stratford, apart from Silvers as I felt I had really settled down now.

'Come on you miserable bugger!' Kay pulled me up from the chair. 'Let's dance.' Joan and Gordon jived past us waving their hands in the air. 'Ah ah ah ah, Ah ah ah ah; at the hop,' their off-key singing drowning Danny and the Juniors. During the course of the evening Mrs Igglesden had been plied with various concoctions of alcohol and had been laid down on a bench by the gallant Mr Delarue, whilst poor old Don, who had probably consumed twice as much as her, was being helped up on to the raised boards to receive his burnished fireman's axe, as a memento of his career, from the Deputy Chief Officer, Bill Baker. Don removed his glasses and wiped an emotional tear from his eye as his trembling hand grasped the coveted symbol of his thirty years' service. The burst of spontaneous applause as he raised the trophy above his head was too much for the poor old bugger and the tears started to stream down his face. Vic tried to rally Vera from the bench to join in the singing of 'For he's a jolly good fellow', but she was totally unplayable and was snoring like a pig. The guys from his watch at Silvertown had kept pace with Don in the consumption of vast quantities of Guinness and whisky chasers and were in no state to help him home.

'We had better take them home,' said Jeff.

'No, it's all right, I'll take them, you'll want to help clear up.' The reflection from the crisp whiteness of Tom's dress shirt was dazzling as he bent down and gently lifted Vera into his arms. 'I'll take her, if you two can bring Don over to my car.'

Don was sitting slumped up against the bay doors, still crying and murmuring the refrain of the last song, 'We'll meet again'.

'Come on, old son, let's get you in Tom's car.' I pulled him up and placed his arm over my shoulder. Jeff grabbed his other arm and we made our way out into the yard.

'Hold on boys, I want a roll-up.' He fell backwards against the wall taking us with him.

'For fuck's sake Don! It's pissing down, wait till you're in the car.'

'Jim.' He steadied himself against the wall as I waited for the rest of his sentence. 'Jim.' He stopped again as he pulled the tin of Nut Brown from his pocket. 'I've got to tell you this, Jim.' We waited expectantly as he opened the tin and took the packet of Rizla fag papers out.

'Yeah, what do you want to tell us, Don?' said Jeff.

Don turned towards Jeff, somewhat startled. 'Hello, Jeff, where did you come from?' His speech was by now very slurred.

'Let me roll that for you,' Jeff tried to take the tobacco and papers away.

''Sall right, I'm not pissed, I can do it.'

He managed to get some tobacco into the paper and then he attempted to lick the gummed edge. His tongue was searching frantically at one corner of his mouth, whilst the fag paper was at the other corner. He lowered the fag down, took a deep breath, grimaced and farted. 'Beg pardon,' he burped. He made another abortive attempt to lick the paper and then despairingly shoved it towards Jeff to roll.

'Jim,' he started once again, 'you and Jeff are my bestest two mates.'

'Yeah, all right Don, come on, let's get you home.'

Jeff stuck the fag into Don's mouth as we struggled towards the car. He stopped dead once more, pulling us off balance.

'Sodding thing's not alight,' he stammered. He delved into his pocket and handed me the lighter. He took the cigarette from his mouth and tried to hold it as steady as he could between his two fingers. Jeff grabbed his wrist so that I could get somewhere near the fag. I flipped the silver top back and thumbed the wheel. The ensuing explosion seared through the cigarette, blasted past Don's nose, sealed his eyelids and cremated his eyebrows on the way to his cap. 'For fuck's sake!' I dropped the red-hot lighter to the ground as the second-degree burns started to appear on my hand.

Don was desperately trying to contort his face muscles in order to prise open his eyes as the combined smell of burning hair and the wool from his cap wafted into his inflamed nostrils.

'Poxy lighter.' He stared down, with the one eye he had managed to open, at the smouldering butt hanging from his lips. He tried desperately to drag on what was left of the cigarette but to no avail. We had now reached the car and were about to shove him into the back seat alongside the snoring Vera, when he stopped abruptly once more and pulled us closer to him. 'Seriously though,' he slurred, 'I want to tell you this, in all sincisity.'

'I think you mean sincerity, Don.'

'That's right, Jeff, sincisery, it's just between us now.' He paused again.

'Come on, Don, what is it?'

He pulled us even closer 'In all sincisity, I think I've shit meself!' The pungent smell drifting up towards us confirmed that he had indeed shit himself. We bundled him into the car before Tom realised what was going on, and hastily waved him out of the yard.

'Very nice of you, Tom, see you when you get back.' I tried to hold the laughter back until Tom's magnificent leather-upholstered Rover 90 had passed the station gate and was out of sight.

'Jesus, he'll go bloody spare when he gets back,' said Jeff as we burst into gales of uncontrollable laughter.

Later the wicket gate to the appliance bay burst open. Tom's face was fire-engine red with rage as he staggered towards us, ripping his bow tie off and loosening his collar. 'You rotten pair of bastards, you knew he'd shit hisself,' he yelled at us. 'I've had to drive back with all the bloody windows open, I'm bloody well frozen.'

Gordon put a consoling arm around Tom's shoulder and guided him away, before he could inflict possible physical damage on us.

Chapter Eight

'White watch, 'shun, for your duties, fall out.' We dutifully clicked our heels in acknowledgement of the sub's orders, turned in unison to the right and made our way to the appliances.

'Could be a long night tonight, Hooligan.' Jeff's assessment wasn't particularly brilliant, as even I had tumbled that Guy Fawkes night was going to be busy.

'They're going to have a TL at Stratford when the takeover comes, Alan.' Fireman Cobb nodded to Vic as if resigned to the fact that he would definitely be going to Stratford as a TL operator.

'It's *not* a takeover, Evans,' Bert said sarcastically. 'It's an *amalgamation*.'

'They're splitting the brigades up into three areas. Chopper's going to be in charge of one,' said Bob Annis.

'Where do you get your information from?' Jeff looked at the mess man quizzically.

'The little bugger's got his head so far up Silvers's arse, he hears it before anyone,' joked Bert. It was common knowledge that Bob had a penchant for sneaking into the 'guv'nor's' office and delving through the latest bulletins.

We entered the mess room and Daisy took the brown enamel tea pot off the gas. He started to pour the stewed brew into the cups just as the bells went down.

'By the looks of that, I didn't want it anyway,' said Jeff as we ran into the yard towards the appliance bay.

'Bonfire, unattended, out of control, pump only,' shouted Ken Smith as he emerged from the watch room.

'Sub, you ride the pump for the remainder of the watch.' Silvers handed the call slip to Bert.

'Bloody good, ain't it, I'll be up all sodding night riding that.'

'Never mind, Bert, you've got me and Hooligan to look after you,' gibed Jeff. The sub-officer was in a foul mood and it just happened there was a full moon tonight.

'He'll need watching tonight,' said Vic as he started the Dennis's engine.

'Bollocks!' Bert pulled his helmet down hard on his head and fastened the leather chinstrap.

'Try not to fall into any cesspits, Sub,' shouted Dave, as he pulled on the rope to open the bay doors.

'Arseholes!' Bert pulled the window up as we moved off.

'Wonder where he learnt the ancient art of repartee?'

'You two tarts can shut up as well.' Bert was in the process of turning towards us in the back when Vic violently slammed the brakes on to avoid a Morris Traveller, whose driver hadn't seen us emerging from the station. Bert shot forward, striking his head against the wooden window stanchion. As his head rocked back once more we could see blood splattered across the windscreen.

'I think you've cut your nose, Sub.' Bert pulled his silk from his tunic and pressed it against his nose.

'Thank you, O'Halloran; it's patently obvious I've cut me fucking nose, thanks to this prat.' He mumbled through the silk at Evans.

'You were so busy effing and blinding at everyone, you didn't ring the bells.'

'Jesus. You can't miss a bloody great fire engine. He must be blind.' Bert tried to shift the blame on to the motorist. 'Wanker!' he yelled at the unsuspecting driver of the Traveller as we sped past him on our way to the Keir

Hardie estate. The bonfire had nearly burnt itself out; we were in the throes of turning over the remains and damping them down when a small boy approached us from the direction of one of the tower blocks.

'Oi, Mister, someone's just thrown a cat from the eighth floor. It ain't dead, it's still wrigglin'.'

'What's he want?' I explained the situation to Bert. 'Put a call though to the RSPCA.'

'Can't you do sumpfing, Mister?' pleaded the boy, who had by now been joined by about ten of his mates.

'Yeah; you're the bleedin' fire brigade, ain't yer?' said a scruffy little urchin who was obviously the gang spokesman by the way admiring glances were being thrown his way by the two little girls in tow.

'Make one of the reels up, Evans, and stay here with the pump, otherwise these little bastards will strip it bare.' One of the 'little bastards' stuck two fingers up to Bert as we made our way round to Ronan Point.

The cat was still alive, just, but obviously beyond saving. Its head had been crushed on one side, its back broken, and it was bleeding heavily from the back passage.

'Oh Jesus, we'd better kill it,' said Bert, looking directly at me and Jeff, implying that he meant us.

'What's all this "we" Tonto; you want it dead – you kill it!'

'I can't do it,' squirmed Bert apologetically.

'No good looking at me,' said Jeff, as he walked away from the writhing cat.

'Looks like you then, Hooligan, see you back at the pump when you've finished.'

The sub-officer turned and sprinted after Jeff.

'Hold on!' I bellowed, as their silhouettes disappeared into the steam and smoke from the bonfire. 'Bastards!'

The 'gang leader' looked directly into my eyes. "Ow you gonna do it, Mister?' Bloody good question, I thought to myself.

'Go on, bugger off,' I walked towards them, gesturing and pushing the kids away from the stricken animal. I managed to get them on to the pavement away from the tower block, but it was evident they intended to move no further. I turned back towards the cat and took a deep intake of air as I knelt down beside it. I fumbled my axe from the leather pouch. The blade was certainly sharp enough to sever the cat's neck in one well-aimed blow. The axe swung from above my head, down past my shoulder and was gathering momentum, when the little girl's scream brought my arm action to a juddering deflection, causing sparks to fly off the paving stone as the axe blade bludgeoned a groove into the forecourt.

'I told you lot to bugger off, didn't I?' I yelled, waving my axe at the kids. The manic arm-waving and expressions must have frightened the living daylights out of them as they scattered in all directions.

The cat's one good eye was now transfixed and staring at me, pleading to end its miserable predicament. Oh shit, how am I going to do this? My mind was pulsating with various methods to end its life, some, easier for my conscience than for the cat's imminent demise. Come on, O'Halloran, for Christ's sake kill it! I panicked and pulled my personal line off my belt and lifted the cat's blood-matted head gently off the ground. I wrapped the rope around the cat's neck and pulled on both ends with as much strength as I could muster. I just couldn't look at the cat; I turned my head away, increasing the pressure on the line, causing my arms to shake violently. It seemed an eternity until the gurgling noise finally stopped. I slackened the rope and threw it in utter disgust against the wall of the tower block. I picked the lifeless tabby up gently off the ground and placed it beside the wall of the flats. Someone must own it, although it didn't have a collar. Who in the name of God could just throw a cat from a balcony like that?

'Why didn't you just whack it with your axe?' asked Vic when I returned to the pump.

'You probably caused the cat more pain by strangling the bloody thing.'

I turned sharply on Jeff. 'All right, all right; I know it was stupid, but where were you bloody heroes? I've never killed anything in my life.'

'It wasn't our problem. We were called to a fire.'

'Piss off, Bert.' I pushed past him and slammed the door shut as I got into the engine.

'Joan would kill him when he got home, if he hadn't done something. That right, Jim?'

Jeff's assumption wasn't far off the mark. Both our families had always had cats and dogs, and Joan's father had kept horses at one time to ply his greengrocery trade around the streets of Stratford. I never really understood people's dislike of animals and found Bert's comments hard to comprehend. Perhaps it was because he had no pets himself.

We had our supper at 8 p.m. and had a few shouts to rubbish fires and bonfires, before we turned in at 11 p.m. We settled into our beds, knowing full well that a completely incident-free night was virtually impossible on the 5th November. The inevitable clanging of the dormitory call bell at 1.10 a.m. had us scurrying out of our pits.

'Someone turn the bleeding lights on, I can't find me kacks.' Vic fumbled around on the floor beside his bed for his trousers as I flicked the switch.

'You've got them on, you dopey sod!' shouted Jeff. A wide grin spread across a face which had taken more than its fair share of right uppercuts.

'Looks like we're going on one of Vic's nodding dog tours – it'll take him ages to wake up.' Jeff likened the excessive use of double-declutching and heavy braking we were about to encounter, while Vic tried to co-ordinate his leg movements with the messages from a brain that was still in sleeping mode, to those silly little toy dogs that seemed so popular on the rear window shelf of people's cars.

'Where to?'

'Near the Connaught, just outside the dock gates, timber yard alight.' This was a full attendance with our four machines, Stratford's two, along with the foam tender, and Silvertown's pump and PE.

The area alight was well known to us from many previous visits. During the war years, huge holes had been dug into the soil, about six feet deep, and reinforced concrete anti-tank buttresses built into them. These had long since been removed, but the holes were never filled in, just left to fill of their own accord with rubbish and water.

'Be careful, I don't want to be up all night filling in accident reports,' shouted Silvers. We ran the two and three quarter inch hemp hose out towards the burning stack of timber.

'Make pumps six, old Cobby, and we'll need a hose layer.' Alan Cobb relayed the message to Stratford control and confirmed to Silvers that the message had been sent at 01:16 hours.

'You two get upwind, and on to one of those stacks.' The leading fireman pointed to two stacks that were about fifteen feet high and not at this stage involved in the fire. Jeff and I struggled up on to the pile of stacked timber planks with the hose and hand-controlled branch. Dave Woods connected our hose line up to the pump ready for the order 'water on'. Because of the lack of fire hydrants, our pump had been set-up in a relay with three other machines at intervals along the road to convey the water to the scene, and to enable the pressure to be maintained in order to fight the fire. Every now and then the wind would change, engulfing us in choking smoke and burning embers.

'We'd better put some water on this stack, Jeff, otherwise we'll fry.'

Jeff pulled the heavy hose up from the ground so that I could spray the stack we were standing on. By now we were inhaling more smoke, causing us to choke and spit. Although there were BA sets on the machines, it was considered that they were not needed, as the fire was in the open air. Here go my bloody kippered lungs again. No problem now, I thought, but wait until I'm about sixty and the effects of years of accumulated smoke inhalation takes its toll. If I asked for a set, they'd only take the mickey.

After about two and a half hours, we had the fires under control and had begun to pull the stacks apart with hooks and our bare hands to get to the seat of the fires and dampen down the charred remains. Silvers had returned to Plaistow with the PE, ET, and TL and left McGinty in charge of the incident.

'Guv, DO Baker's just pulled up outside the gates in his car.' From our vantage point we could survey the scene in its entirety.

'Fanks, Hooligan, better warn 'im about the 'oles.' The holes were full of dirty sludge and stagnant water and extremely deep in some places.

'This way, sir, follow me, it's a little bit iffy if you don't know where—' McGinty's instructions were cut abruptly short as both he and the pursuing divisional officer disappeared below the water level of one of the holes. Biff Baker was the first to surface, clutching his undress uniform cap in one hand and his bicycle torch in the other. He spat some grimy sludge out as McGinty's head bobbed up beside him, minus his helmet. The divisional officer was obviously not impressed by Paddy's geographical guidance as he blasted into the cold night air, 'You fucking idiot, McGinty!' The station officer was frantically trying to assist Baker from the hole, but the DO was just as frenziedly pushing his attempts away. 'Piss off! I'll get out myself.' He clambered out of the hole, shivering in the cold night air.

'Serves him right,' said Jeff. Senior officers should wear the proper rig on the fire ground, same as us.' He was right of course; the undress uniform was totally inadequate for scuba diving, but Baker had probably rolled out of a nice warm bed and wanted to get back to his old woman without the aggravation of rigging in fire gear. He followed McGinty to the burning stacks, his undress trousers slowly slipping from his waist due to the extra weight of the water. He hoisted them up angrily, grunting towards the still apologising station officer.

'You won't need any reliefs on this job,' he said threateningly. 'I think I can even leave you to tie this one up.' He turned sharply to get back to his Ford Consul.

'Eh, 'scuse me, Guv, this way.' Baker gave another tug of his trousers, slammed the wringing wet cap on to his head and scowled at McGinty.

'Fuck off! I'll find my own bleeding way back.' He wiped the mud from his face with his hanky and stormed back towards the road. He had only travelled a few feet when the ground opened up beneath him once again. This time the torch was a goner, but fortunately the cap stayed afloat. Once again, Baker's head broke through the surface like Excalibur rising from the lake, turning from side to side, maniacally searching for the unfortunate station officer. 'You cunt, McGinty!' he screamed, banging his fist down on to the gunge, causing a spiral of oozing mud to cascade down on to him.

'But sir, I did say—'

McGinty was sliced into silence by a vicious swipe of an outstretched index finger, missing his nose by inches. 'Shut it! Just shut it, don't say another fucking word!' Baker's face was now threateningly close to Paddy's. McGinty shrugged his shoulders apologetically. The divisional officer gave a final tug to his ever-weightier trousers and squelched his way with his one remaining shoe to the car. The slamming of the door could probably be heard all over Beckton.

'What are you two lying down for?' I tried to answer Bert, but couldn't get my breath, because of the uncontrollable bout of laughter we had lapsed into.

Bert turned towards Vic, who wasn't much better, sliding down the side of the pump into a quivering heap. The sub held his stern countenance for as long as he could before he, too, fell down on all fours, grabbing Evans for support.

We were relieved by the PE at 5.30 a.m., swapped machines and returned to the station. We had time for a quick shower before the bells went down again to return us to Ronan Point. It appeared someone had enjoyed our performance earlier and wanted to see us again.

'Send back Malicious, old Cobby, you'd think the little bastards would be in bed at this time,' spat Silvers, assuming our little gang was still on the prowl. We pulled ourselves wearily back on to the engines in time to hear Frank Griffiths at Stratford Control ordering us on to a bomb fire unattended at the back of Samson Street Hospital.

'We ain't going to get back in our pits tonight, boys,' proffered Vic. Needless to say, he was right. We finished the shift knackered but defiant.

Chapter Nine

'The kid's soundo, I've never known a kid to sleep like that.' Joan and I had just returned from the Rex-Stratford after watching John Wayne – for once, not a cowboy – in *The Magnificent Showman* with the latest Hollywood pin-up, Claudia Cardinale.

'Thanks, Dad.'

Percy had come over to babysit Corinne on his own, as Amy had to finish her outdoor work, as a hand finisher of ladies' dresses.

'She been all right?' I asked.

'Good as gold, no trouble at all. As long as she's got something to eat, she's as happy as a sandboy.'

'I hope you've not been spoiling her,' said Joan.

Percy smiled. We knew that all her grandparents and great-grandparents spoiled her something rotten. We were fortunate to live about equal distance from both Joan's parents in Forest Gate and my mother and her parents in Goodmayes. Corinne's other surviving great-grandmother lived in Finchley.

Percy tied his scarf around his neck in the time-honoured fashion of the costermonger, slipped his heavy duty raincoat on and pushed his moped out of the front garden into the road. 'Thanks, Dad,' shouted Joan as she closed the wooden gate. 'Mind how you go.'

'Gordon and Kay are thinking of moving to Southend,' I said as Joan sat down, beating me to the armchair closest to the open coal fire. 'You've dropped something.' I pointed back towards the door and thudded into the now vacant chair as Joan looked for the imaginary something.

'That's what you think,' she said, pulling at my arm. 'Come on, that's my chair.' I grabbed her waist and drew her on to my lap. 'Come on, then, we'll share.'

'Why Southend?'

'Don't know, really, except that property's a lot cheaper down there.'

'They're buying it?' Joan said, somewhat surprised.

'That's what Gordon told me. Christ knows how they can afford the mortgage, though.'

'How much is the house, then?'

'It's detached, about four grand, I think he said.'

'I think Kay's got relatives down that way somewhere.' Joan suddenly became thoughtful. I squeezed her waist gently.

'What's up mate?'

'It's going to be quiet without Kay. We really get on well together.'

That was an understatement. They had been described by the chief officer as 'formidable'. It was certainly going to change our social life. Kay and Gordon would be sadly missed.

'Look on the bright side mate, maybe we will move soon.'

'You've got to be joking; how can we afford a mortgage?'

Joan was right; our income wouldn't improve much until I got promoted or after fifteen years I would receive a long service increment.

'You never know, kiddo,' I sighed. 'Give us a kiss.' Joan pressed her lips against mine but her mind was as far away from romance. As for our chances of buying a house, Steve, our lodger, had already left to work in Surrey somewhere, which reduced our income even more.

'Fire needs some coal.'

I took the coal scuttle from the hearth and went out through the back door down a small flight of concrete steps into the pitch black garden. I lifted the coal shed lid and started to fill the scuttle, then stopped suddenly. I could hear someone breathing! I turned quickly. Nothing! I strained my head towards the sound. It was coming from my workshed. I put the shovel and scuttle down and made my way gingerly towards the shed. The rasping breathing was louder with each step nearer. 'Anyone there?' I ventured timorously. No reply. I eased the door slowly open. 'Hello?' By now the sound was horrendous, as if the person were asthmatic or in the last throes of dying. It was impossible to see because of the dark. 'Is anybody there?' Jesus, I sound like a bloody medium. The breathing got louder.

Sod this, I'm going for a torch. I rushed back into the house and fumbled in the cupboard under the stairs for the torch.

'You'll wake Corinne up. What's the matter?'

'There's someone in the shed.'

'Someone in the shed?' Joan grabbed my arm protectively. 'Be careful.'

I made my way cautiously towards the shed and tentatively started to prise the door open. 'Be careful,' blurted out Joan who had crept up behind me in her carpet slippers. 'Jesus,' I yelled, dropping the torch on to the ground, 'I wish you wouldn't do that.' I picked the torch up but the fall had obviously broken the bulb. I continued to open the door and felt blindly just inside to the right-hand side for a shovel I knew was there. The breathing was even worse. I grabbed the shovel and dived into the middle of the shed, wielding it above my head like a demented dervish and screaming at the top of my voice. Once all the pent-up fear and exertion had drained from my body, I stood, totally exhausted, in the middle of the shed, awaiting the inevitable attack from the now louder-breathing maniac. I stumbled frantically towards the rasping inhalations, making a despairing grab at where the bastard should be.

'Bollocks!'

'What's the matter?' Joan shouted anxiously.

'I've just smashed my bloody foot on the bench.'

'Who's in there?'

'Nobody,' I replied. 'Can't see a bloody thing, but the breathing's stopped.'

'Leave it, Jim, have a look in the morning when it's light.' I had used up my quota of Dutch courage for the night and wasn't about to argue with Joan to prove my manhood. I limped painfully back through the kitchen and spent the rest of the evening with my swollen foot soaking in water.

★

'What's Daddy done to his foot Mummy?' Corinne said, pointing to my bandaged toe with the spoon from her cornflakes. She had slept soundly through the night as usual, woken up and happily started to demolish her breakfast.

'Don't wave your spoon about. He hurt it in the shed last night.' Once she had satisfied herself that Daddy was okay, she continued with the important job of finishing her meal.

'I looked in the shed first thing this morning, no breathing, nothing, it's really weird.'

'I shouldn't worry,' said Joan. 'Perhaps your fireman ghost, what's his name, Godfrey, has followed you from the old Stratford station.'

'What's a ghost, Daddy?'

'Someone who eats little girls' cornflakes.'

Corinne's face contorted into the start of a crying bout.

'Trust you! Now look what you've done. Daddy's joking, peachy, nobody's going to pinch your cornflakes.' With Joan's reassurance, the tears miraculously stopped and another spoonful of flakes was hastily devoured.

I kissed them both good-bye before riding off to work on my push-bike as the car had been playing up. I had got as far as the Barking Road and had turned into Tunmarsh Lane to avoid the traffic lights at the Green Gate pub, and was about to pass a stationary car when the door flew open. My front wheel crunched into the door as I went cartwheeling over it. The first part of my body to make contact with the concrete was, of course, my bloody foot, as I crashed into the gutter. I rolled over in agony, clutching my foot first, then my battered ribcage. I lay there for a few seconds feeling shocked and thinking things couldn't get worse, but they bloody well did. It started to piss down.

For a few seconds I lay there, winded, but as the shock gradually wore off I started to compose in my head exactly what I was going to call the driver of the Ford Prefect. I hauled myself unsteadily to my feet as he approached me and was just about to commence a barrage of rehearsed abuse when he said, 'What a fucking stupid bastard I am!' My mouth had already started to form the exact same phrase but remained wide open, as I hadn't planned anything else other than that. 'You all right, mate?' I nodded, still mesmerised at having my thunder stolen from me. 'You're not a copper are you?' He had noticed my air force blue brigade shirt, which was identical to those worn by police constables. He began to look even more concerned. I shook my head. 'Thank Christ for that.' Hold on, I thought to myself, so it's all right to knock some poor bugger off his bike, as long as he's not a rozzer.

'I'm a fireman,' I replied, shakily.

'That's all right, then,' he said as he assisted me towards a small brick wall and sat me down. I think I'll hit him. No,

Jim! You were fired from the railway for thumping the foreman; you don't want the sack again.

I grasped my side as I painfully tried to inhale. 'Is your station the one down the road?' He pointed down Prince Regent Lane. 'I'll go and get someone from there for you.' He's not such a bad bloke, I thought, as he drove off down the lane.

As the station was only about a quarter of a mile down the road and a good half hour had elapsed, it started to dawn on me suddenly that I had come up for the five-card trick. I angrily began to regret the fact that the bugger hadn't even let me have the satisfaction of swearing at him.

I put the crumpled remains of my Raleigh Sports into a front garden and made my way to the phone box. I put sixpence into the black metal box, dialled the station and waited for the watch room man to answer. 'Is that you, Smithy?' I queried as I pressed button A. 'I've had an accident. I'm up by the Green Gate; can someone pick me up?'

Bob Annis pulled up beside me in his car. 'Christ, what happened to you, Hooly?' I explained the details as he drove back to the station.

'You'd better get yourself up Samson Street Hospital; old O'Halloran, you're no bloody good to me,' slithered Silvers. 'I don't want to see you until you're fit for duty.'

After the hospital had attended to my bruised ribs and foot, Bob drove me home to Dersingham Avenue. Vic Evans picked my bike up in his van after the shift finished. I milked the sympathy from the situation as far as I was able with Joan, to the point where she volunteered to get the coal in. After a few seconds she dashed back into the dining room. 'That breathing's in the shed again,' she said agitatedly. I leapt up from the armchair, grabbed the torch and tried to run towards the garden, when my ribs reminded me that I was in no fit state to tackle whoever was in the shed. I opened the door gingerly with Joan close behind me. The heavy breathing was coming from the direction of the bench at the back. I shone the torch along the bench and there in the corner under the lower shelf was the culprit. The black and white cat's side was heaving heavily with every gasp of air. His fur was thickly matted and appeared stiff and tacky. Joan rushed back into the house and brought an old blanket out to wrap the poor animal in. The cat made no attempt to run – it was too weak to move. I wrapped the blanket gently around the pitiful creature and lifted him into Joan's arms. 'Where's the nearest vet?'

'Either at the bottom of Ilford Lane or down West Ham Lane,' Joan replied, 'but they'll be shut by now.'

'Yeah, and the bloody car's off the run anyway. I'll go and phone Rosie to see if your brother Bob can drive over – the PDSA are open all night at Ilford.'

I struggled down to the red telephone kiosk outside the off-licence at the bottom of our turning. As Percy and Amy were not on the phone, I had to wait whilst their next door neighbours relayed my message to Bob.

By the time I got back to the house with the news that rescue was imminent, the cat had died.

On the advice of Doctor Shannahan at Forest Gate, I spent the next week resting. Because the car was off the run, this rest entailed lugging huge shopping bags from the top of Romford Road for about a mile to our home or carrying Corinne whilst Joan did the lifting. I was glad to return to work.

I was detailed mess assistant upon my return on our first day duty. This meant that I assisted the female civilian cook by way of peeling vegetables, sweeping floors, laying tables, and washing up. She was a large robust woman in her late fifties with flame-red hair and a temper to match and could more than hold her own in 'discussions' that required a tirade of foul language to prove a point. Rank markings were no guarantee of protection from the sharp end of her tongue. The younger element of the watch were not as familiar as the older hands who appeared to get away with murder when the banter started with her. She was not averse to swinging the odd right-hander or tipping your meal over your head if you dared to complain about her culinary skills.

'How long you been here now?' Vic asked as she wiped the dripping gravy from the side of his plate. 'Twenty-four years,' she replied. 'Why?'

'I just thought that by now you'd have sussed how to cook a bit of steak and kidney,' Vic replied curtly as he ambled back towards the mess table.

'You cheeky bastard.' Before she had even finished the sentence, a large handful of mashed potato was winging its way towards the back of Vic's head. A huge grin spread across his craggy features as he ducked in knowing anticipation of the outcome of his remark. The dollop of mash splattered on to the shiny plastic surface besides Bert's arm.

'Thanks,' said Bert scooping the potato off the table and piling it on to his already overloaded plate. Daisy shook his head in disbelief.

'You're a bleedin' animal, you are, Bert,' the cook shouted as she grabbed a dish cloth to wipe the table.

The sideways rubbing movement caused her huge breasts to swing from side to side as she leant over besides Bert. He continued to fork his meal into his mouth with his right hand whilst his left hand sought cautiously for the nearest of the cook's swinging pendulous orbs. We all sat watching – some of us in awe at the sub-officer's bravado, others in the certain knowledge that retribution would be swift and in all probability, extremely painful. The speed of her hand movement was awe-inspiring as she snapped her hand tightly into Bert's groin and squeezed, causing her knuckles to turn white – not as white, though, as the stricken sub-officers face as he slowly rose from his chair, face contorted and unable to shriek because of the vice-like grip being applied to his testicles. Bert grabbed frantically with both hands to the underside of the table as his chair clattered to the stone floor from the involuntary action of his jerking leg.

'All right, all right,' he screamed as the cook put her full sixteen-odd stone into overdrive on the task in hand. 'Me nuts, me nuts, for Christ's sake,' he yelled, grabbing the cook's arm to try and relieve the pain.

'What the fucking hell's going on here, old Cross?' The stocky silhouette of Silvers stood out as the winter sun shone through the now open mess room door.

'Nothing, Guv,' replied the cook, as she released her grip on Bert's wedding tackle. 'Bert was just complimenting me on my cooking, weren't you, Sub?'

The station officer glanced at the doubled-up figure on the floor who was trying both to massage between his legs and answer at the same time. 'Mmm, mmm.'

'Don't sound too convincing to me, old Cross,' Silvers beamed. I know she's not a bad cook, but praising her on your knees! I think you're going overboard a bit there, Sub,' The cook helped to lift the stricken sub-officer up off the floor and assisted him back into his seat.

'You all right, Bert?' She leant over and affectionately left her lipstick imprint on to Bert's receding hairline. Bert smiled gently through the pain and patted the cook's backside as she walked back into the kitchen to serve the station officer.

After dinner (it didn't become lunch until much later in the East End) I started to strip the double-ovened gas cooker down, whilst the cook washed up humming happily to herself. It started out with 'Younger than Springtime' and then I was to suffer a random selection from various musicals.

'Don't you know any Jerry Lee Lewis, or Chuck Berry?'
I pleaded hopefully.

'Bleedin' wog music, bang bang bang, that's all that shit
is.'

Oh well, that seemed to exhaust that channel of her
musical appreciation; not much point discussing the
Mersey sound, I thought, as that would be deemed to be a
bunch of long-haired scouse gits, banging away again. I just
had to accept that our cook was somewhat insular in her
musical taste. It was no good complaining – I could end up
like poor old Bert!

The shrill clanging of the call bell had the dual effect of
me banging my head on the roof of the oven as I tried to get
up off my knees and the cook dropping a plate back into the
stainless steel sink. 'Jesus, I'll never get used to that bloody
thing,' she said, fishing around in the sink to retrieve the
plate. 'Go on, Hooligan, I'll finish off in here.'

'Where's the magical mystery tour this time, Smithy,' I
said, rubbing the top of my head briskly before I stuck my
helmet on.

'Stratford's ground, Queen Mary's Hospital down West
Ham Lane.'

'A fire?'

'Nah, special service, details a bit iffy.'

'Iffy?'

Ken shrugged his shoulders as he struggled into his fire
tunic. 'Guv'nor knows all about it, apparently.'

Normally the ET would have attended a special service
call along with Stratford's appliances, but as they were
attending another incident, our pump and pump escape had
been ordered, but why all the secrecy?

'You lot stay here until I call for you,' Silvers ordered
adjusting his insecure dentures. 'You follow me, Sub.'

We waited expectantly by the main entrance doors. It
couldn't be anything serious, otherwise why were we here,

outside? Bert emerged with an enormous grin on his face, shaking his head in disbelief. 'Right, we don't want all of you; O'Halloran, Daisy, fetch the hearth kit in. You're going to love this Woodsie – oh, and leave your helmets off, you won't need them, we don't want to frighten the patients.' I grabbed the hearth kit off the pump, shrugged my shoulders at my bemused comrades and ran off after Bert and Daisy. (There must be a music hall act in that pairing somewhere?) We followed the sub into the accident and emergency operating theatre where we were confronted by two doctors, their nursing assistants and our station officer peering bemusedly at the outstretched patient on the operating table. As Sid stood to one side, the full complexity of the patient's dilemma manifested itself.

'How the fuck—'

I was cut short in mid sentence. 'Don't even think of asking, old O'Halloran.'

'You reckon none of your tools will cut it, then?' Bert asked one of the doctors.

'No, our stuff's made to cut flesh and bones only.'

Silvers opened the hearth kit, slowly perusing the tools inside. He shook his head in disappointment. 'Nope, nothing here.' He scratched his head. 'Go and tell the ET crew to bring their cutting gear in, old Woodsie.' There was a lengthy silence. 'Oh Christ, he hasn't gone again!' The station officer spun round to confront Dave, who was staring down at the steel ring spanner, painfully embedded at the base of the swollen penis.

'Woodsie!'

'Oh. Yes, okay Guv.' Fireman Woods emerged from his trance-like state and made for the door.

'And tell them they don't have to rig in fire gear.' Bert shouted after him. Surprisingly, the man wasn't making as much noise as I would have anticipated, probably more from embarrassment than anything.

'You're not going to believe this,' Dave blurted to the ET crew as he went on to describe in graphic detail the task they were about to face. 'Oh and no fire gear.'

'So what's the rig, then?' the mystified Alan Cobb demanded on behalf of the crew.

'You can wear what you like, but I'm putting these bastards on,' replied Jeff as he opened the black tin box containing the thick, vulcanised rubber gloves normally used for electrical incidents. He shook the white powder in which they were stored off the long gauntlet gloves before stretching them over his hands, then he grabbed a two foot-long pair of bolt-croppers from the side locker of the appliance and marched off with Evans and Cobb, who were struggling with the cylinders and torch from the portable hot cutting trolley. The swing doors burst open as they cluttered into the operating theatre with the tools of their trade.

'For Christ's sake, that's a bit over the top – you'll scare the poor sod to death, old Cobby.'

The patient stared fixedly at the torture implements being laid down on the floor beside the bed. 'We'll try some more of that jelly stuff you've got there, Doc, before we revert to more drastic measures,' said Silvers. 'Here, old Woodsie, rub some of this on his old boy; I'll try to wiggle the spanner.'

'*Me?*' Dave looked horrified. He gingerly squeezed the gel from the tube on to his index finger.

'Come on, Woodsie, for Christ's sake, we'll be here all bloody day otherwise,' said Bert, grabbing the foreskin between his thumb and finger and holding the penis upright to assist the application.

Daisy's face contorted into a grimace as he rubbed the gel on to the swollen red and mauve welt at the base of the member. The man groaned as Silvers tried to get some movement from the spanner. 'No, it's not going to move;

we'll have to cut it off.' The panic-stricken patient had to be reassured by the doctor that the station officer was referring to the spanner and not his watch and chain.

'Bolt-croppers, Guv?' Jeff raised the huge steel cutters up off the floor.

'No, too dicey, it's going to have to be the old hacksaw, I'm afraid.'

'He's afraid! Imagine what that poor sod feels like,' I whispered to Vic.

'It's really swollen up above the spanner,' muttered Alan through clenched teeth.

'Looks like a lazy lob,' added Vic.

'I'm surprised Bert hasn't suggested tossing him off.' Vic chuckled at my remark. 'Yeah, the thought had crossed my mind, too.'

'Put that gear down and give us a hand over here, you three.' The nasal twang of Silvers's voice jolted us into response to his orders.

The plan of attack was that whilst the station officer carefully cut a groove into the steel ring with the hacksaw, Jeff and I would try to prise the weakened ring open by pulling it apart with pliers. Vic would pour water on to the ring to prevent heat build-up from the friction of the two metals.

Dave was quite happy to be relieved of his duty, whilst Bert remained in a state of euphoria at his given task. I've never seen a man relish someone else's misfortune with such obvious delight. He probably wouldn't wash his hand for a week! No matter how careful, we were unable to prevent further skin damage and abrasions to the ever-discolouring, swollen penis. 'Sorry mate, we're almost there.' The man smiled at me apologetically, waving his hand as if urging us on. 'I can't cut any deeper, I'll be cutting his old boy – give it another tug with the pliers.' We made one concerted effort and the ring snapped apart. The patient jerked forward in pain and relief, his hands shooting down to soothe the throbbing member.

'All yours now, Doc,' said Silvers as we gathered up our gear and made our way back to the engines.

'All right, Guv, you can tell us now. How in the name of Christ did he get that on there?'

Silvers's deformed lip curled into a semblance of a smile as he told us that the story was the guy was having it away with this woman when her husband came home early with his brother, found the two copulating and dragged the guy down to the shed, where they worked the ring spanner on to his dick.

'And you believe that, do you, Sid?' said Bert mischievously. Silvers shrugged his shoulders as he climbed up into the Merryweather and puzzled over the format his stop message would take. He adjusted his dentures, anticipating a few problems with 'spanner' and 'penis' and decided to send a 'details to follow' stop, allowing him to return to the station to work on a suitable paraphrase to that offered by Bert's ambiguous suggestion. 'Tool stuck in tool, tool damaged, removed.'

★

We arrived back at the station where Bert took great pleasure in showing the cook the unwashed forefinger and thumb of his right hand whilst going into graphic detail of the incident. 'You lying sod, he's lying, ain't 'e Jim?'

''Fraid not, it's the truth.'

Her whole body shook uncontrollably as the sub-officer went into even greater depth at the poor sod's misfortune. She wiped the tears away from her ever-reddening cheeks with her pinafore. 'Oh Christ, I've got to sit down.' She collapsed into the chair, hanging on to Bert's arm for support.

'I don't think it's that funny,' Daisy said indignantly, taking a bite out of some apple pie left over from dinner.

'Have you washed your hands, old Woodsie?' said Silvers, as if deeply concerned.

'Oh Christ!' Dave dropped the pie on to the table and rushed out across the drill yard in the direction of the ablutions, much to the merriment of the watch.

Jeff and I made our way over to the dormitory where we were to continue with our station cleaning duties by laying a thick coating of orange-coloured polish on to the floor and then bumping it up to a mirror-like shine with what can only be described as a padded oblong leaded weight about twelve inches by six, attached to a loose-levered broom handle. I put my full weight behind the bumper as I pushed it forward over the drying polish. Dave Woods entered the room to get to his locker. 'Oi, Daisy, get off the floor,' shouted Jeff.

'Just want to get my book to read in the watch room.' I had noticed the book before, simply because of its thickness and the fact that Vic seemed unusually interested in Fireman Wood's progress with the book. 'What's it about, Daisy?'

'Science fiction, actually, a bit like Bert's account of that job – it's really good, though.' He disappeared through the door which led into the appliance room and made his way to the watch room, clutching the book to his side.

'It'll take him weeks to read that book.'

'Yeah, Vic said there's five hundred and sixty-two pages in it,' replied Jeff. I stopped pushing the bumper and tried to remember having seen Vic reading that book, or indeed any book, apart from the Ring. 'How does he know that, then?'

'I dunno,' Jeff took his ciggy tin from out of his overall pocket and proceeded to roll a fag. Leading Fireman Rice entered from the ablutions door, marched up towards us and declared that providing the guv'nor was satisfied after inspecting the station work, we would be stood down after 15:00 hours – in other words, the remainder of the watch, until 18:00 hours would be free time, to do as we please.

'Thanks, Wally,' said Jeff sarcastically. 'We won't be finished at six o'clock, if you keep walking over the bloody floor.' The leading fireman tried to retrace his steps, systematically, apologising profusely for the large imprints left on the floor.

The large call bell above my head clattered the alarm that we wouldn't be standing-down, no matter how quickly we finished the floor. The red and green lights in the middle of the bay were alight as the drivers of the pump and pump escape revved the engines whilst we scrambled aboard. The row of different coloured lights, indicating which appliances had been ordered, were duplicated in the drill yard and instigated a mocking cheer from the members of the ET and TL.

'On your way, boys, don't work too hard!' Alan Cobb jumped up and grabbed hold of the large rope hanging from the system of pulleys which opened the folding wooden bay doors. He yanked it downwards and waved us out of the station.

'Shed alight, somewhere along the Northern Outfall,' Silvers shouted above the noise of the engine pulsating under the cowling in the cab. The Northern Outfall sewer straddled West Ham from Stratford in the west of the borough down to Barking pumping station which was on Essex ground and was one of the largest sewers in London. At some stages it ran above or at ground level and would form a sixteen foot wide path along its route. Access was gained from various roads in the borough via large spiked iron gates and spiked iron fencing stretched along its course, protecting the sloping embankments from trespassers. It ran through large areas of unkempt open land that were either used as dumps, allotments or camps by travelling people. (Bert insisted they were some of my relatives, Irish tinkers.) We turned left off Prince Regent Lane and drove through the open gates on to the sewer path. In actual fact, the gates and fence had long since ceased to be a deterrent to the locals who used the route as a short cut across the borough. A pillar of tarry black smoke billowed from the roof of a corrugated tin shed at the bottom of the embankment.

'Might not have enough water 'ere, Guv.' Silvers acknowledged Bert's assessment. 'We'll see how we go.'

I climbed up on to the top of the pump and handed the two six foot scaling ladders down to Ken Smith. He placed one against the iron railing, climbed to the top with the other ladder, lowered it down the bank side of the fence and secured both ladders to the top of the fencing. Bert took his crew over the fence and we handed them the rolled lengths of hose as they made their way to the shed.

The six lengths of fifty foot hose were hastily connected as they ran towards the blazing roof. 'We need one more length, Hooligan,' shouted the sub-officer above the crackling roar of the orange and black clouds erupting from the shed. I clambered over the ladders and dropped down the sloping embankment, ready for Dave to throw the rolled length over to me. He struggled up the scaling ladder with the heavy hose on his shoulder, placed one leg astride the fence on to the other ladder and grunted as the hose was heaved down towards me. The thud must have obscured Daisy's first cry for help but the second scream did the trick. I looked up to see Fireman Woods in a sitting position on the fence. Christ, it looked as though he'd got his leggings caught on the spikes.

'Be with you in a minute, Dave.' I passed the hose to the leading fireman and struggled back up the embankment.

Dave was trying to lift himself up but appeared to be well and truly stuck. I reached out towards him.

'No, no, don't pull me, Jim.' The sheer expression of pain on Daisy's drained face made me realise that it wasn't just his black leggings that had been punctured.

'All right, Dave, don't panic, mate, let's see what you've done.' I lifted the back of his woollen fire tunic up and saw the blood trickling down the black painted spike, that was impaled by a good three inches into his buttocks.

'All right, Daisy, keep absolutely still until we can take your weight off the fence.' The pump operator, Ken Smith, had run from the pump with the first-aid box.

'Hold him under the arms, Ken, get some weight off if we can.' Dave yelled out as Ken ascended the ladder and gently placed his arms under him.

'Okay, Daisy, you're going to be all right,' said Ken reassuringly. By now, the others had spotted us and quickly realised we were in trouble.

'What the fuck's he done now?' panted Bert as he scrambled up the grass slope.

'He's got a railing stuck up his arse,' replied Smudge, pointing to the blood-soaked dungarees.

'Order the ET on, Bert.' The station officer realised that the cutting gear in the hearth set, apart from the trusty hacksaw, would take ages to get Fireman Woods off the railings.

The ET came rumbling along the dirt track road, blue lights flashing and bells ringing, lurching from side to side under the extra weight it carried for special services such as this. The box-shaped appliance screeched to a halt. The back door flew open and the crew disembarked, carrying the oxyacetylene cutting gear.

'Christ, Daisy, 'ow the bleedin' 'ell did you do that?'

'It wasn't too difficult, Vic,' replied Dave through gritted teeth.

Fireman Evans pulled the petrol lighter from his overall trousers and flicked the wheel. Alan Cobb opened the regulating valve slowly as the volatile mixture of gases exploded into a piercing blue roaring flame. He pulled the protective goggles over his eyes as he moved towards the stricken fireman.

'It's all right, Daisy, just relax, we'll soon have you off there.'

The apprehension on Dave's face was not entirely without reason, as he had seen this awesome piece of equipment in use many times when cutting casualties out of cars. A large asbestos sheet was placed between his leg and the offending spike to prevent burns, whilst a hose-reel was played on to the fence as Alan began cutting. 'Put your weight on to the ladder with your right leg, Dave, it'll help Cobby a bit.'

Daisy frowned at me. 'Sod Cobby, just get me off of here.' I think it was the first time I'd ever heard Dave swear. The pain was obviously getting to him now. 'Here comes the ambulance, Dave, won't be long now,' said a deeply concerned Ken Smith.

'I've always said you were a pain in the arse, Woodsie, now you've proved it.' Fireman Woods feigned a smile at the sub-officer. 'And you haven't fainted!'

'Right, take his weight you two,' shouted Alan, as he burnt through the remaining piece of rail. We lifted him gently down and carried him into the ambulance, laying him down on his side with the protruding spike uppermost.

'Looks worse than it is,' said the ambulance man, reassuring Dave as he placed a large wound dressing around the rail. 'They'll soon have that out.'

'You go with him, old Cobby. You'll have to get a bus back – we haven't got enough riders.' The station officer thought that this would upset Alan, but had forgotten that the laconic Fireman Cobb would not react with the same emotion as one the younger hands, such as myself; he would in all probability turn the situation to his own advantage by stringing it out and claiming overtime. Alan winked at me as he closed the doors as if to confirm my suspicion. I chuckled out loud.

'Problem, old O'Halloran?' Silvers had evidently realised what Alan would do and was now going to pick on me.
'No, Guv, no problems.'

'Well, get *your* arse over that fence, and help put that bloody shed out – see if you think that's funny,' he sneered.

'What was that all about, Jim?' asked Jeff as we got up-wind of the smoke and started to pour water on to the shed roof. I shrugged my shoulders in ignorance.

'He's just a nasty little bastard,' mumbled Vic as he went with Bert to break the lock off the door. 'It won't open outwards, Sub, there's a bloody great iron girder sunk into the ground.'

'Well kick the bleedin' thing in, then.'

Vic leaned back and put his full weight behind the effort. The ensuing dull thud reverberated through his leather boots, juddering the entire bone structure in his leg. He fell backwards, clutching his knee. 'Jesus fuckin' Christ, I've done me soddin' leg in.' He rolled about in agony as Bert walked towards him.

'What's up now, for Christ's sake?' screamed Silvers.

'Evans has done his leg in, Guv,' Bert lifted Vic up under his arms and sat him on an old crate. 'I'll be all right in a minute, Sub,' Vic winced, rubbing his knee slowly.

'Surrounded by a bunch of bleedin' old tarts, I am. 'Ere, I'll show you 'ow to knock a soddin' door in.' The sub-officer looked somewhat cumbersome as he stooped down as if ready to begin a four-minute mile assault on the offending door. His boots, which were seemingly one size too big, clattered against the hard ground as he gathered momentum. By now he had covered a good twenty yards and the slight twist of his torso confirmed that overdrive was now the mode and that the brain was totally disengaged. His eyes had taken on a strange transfixed stare and his arms seemed to be pumping in time to the predetermined beat of what for Bert could only be 'Bad Moon Rising'. The lights were definitely out! Flesh and bone were about to explode on the ill-fated wooden door. Bert's whole body was in mid-air as his shoulder smashed into the door at full throttle. In fairness, it has to be said that the door did move slightly inwards before it sprung back into its original stubborn position. The horrendous whooshing sound could be heard quite clearly as the breath extruded from Bert's lungs. He came back off the door in a slow motion arc and landed with a sickening thump on to the hard ground surrounding the shed.

'You all right, Bert?' Jeff and I ran towards the stricken sub-officer.

'Fer... fer... fer...' His efforts to say something cohesive were being hampered by what could only be compared to a very bad asthma attack.

'Fah... fah...' he gallantly continued, trying to force the obscenities out between large gulps of air.

'Fuck it? Is that what you're trying to say Bert?'

Bert nodded agreement at me as we started to lift him off the ground. He yelled out in pain as I grabbed his armpit. 'Kuh... kuh...' he wheezed at me as we helped him to sit on an old empty oil drum. He gulped the air back into his lungs and waited patiently until he was able to call me by repeated use of his favourite four-letter expletive, adding the occasional reference to my Celtic ancestry. Silvers came running around from the back of the shed. 'What the hell's happened now?'

'I think the sub-officer may have injured his shoulder, Guv.'

'Christ, it's beginning to look like a bloody battlefield. Why won't the door open, then?'

I shrugged my shoulders, 'Don't know, Guv.'

'Go and get the crowbar off the pump, old O'Halloran.' Silvers paused and then shouted after me, 'and for Christ's sake don't fall arse over tip on that fence.' I panted my way back towards the shed and made my way to the door.

'Here, give it to me.' The station officer snatched the steel bar from my hands. 'We can't afford another casualty.' He smashed the chiselled end between the door and the frame, placing one leg against the shed to give him the extra leverage he required. The squat figure put his full twelve-stone body weight behind the effort, his short neck seeming to sink ever further into his shoulders. 'Don't just stand there, you two, give us a hand.' Jeff and I placed our hands on the crowbar and began pulling. A loud crack echoed above the noise of the fire as part of the door finally succumbed to our concerted assault. We all three, still had hold of the bar as the resistance was instantly released, causing us to tumble into a heap upon one another.

'Watch the side!' Bert bellowed. I rolled over on to my back in time to see the whole wooden side panel of the shed cascading down towards us, followed by a mountain of burning rubber car tyres. I was in the process of raising myself off the ground when the first of what seemed to be an endless bombardment of the bloody things thumped into the small of my back.

'Your tunic's alight, Hooligan,' Ken Smith shouted as he pointed to my back and began spraying water on to me from the hose.

'Sod this for a game of soldiers,' I frantically pulled at the buttons on my tunic. The two existing casualties had momentarily forgotten their injuries and were evidently enjoying the frantic spectacle of us trying to evade the blazing tyres, at the same time urging Smithy to make more use of the hose.

'Well, at least we know why the bloody door wouldn't open – the place was packed tight with the sodding things,' Vic mused, still rubbing the knee which had swollen up considerably.

'You all right, Guv?' Bert asked, still trying to lift his arm to relieve the pain from his shoulder. Silvers raised himself off the ground, holding his right hand over his face. 'Something's got into my eye.' Jeff pulled his hand from his face and peered into his eye. 'Can't see anything, but it looks nasty.'

'Looks like Chiefy's here, Guv.' Ken pointed towards the Zephyr hurtling along the embankment. Cutting had been informed by control that Daisy had been taken to hospital and obviously wanted to know the circumstances, but hadn't expected to be greeted by the array of first-aid boxes and casualties now before him.

'What the fucking hell is going on here, Silvers. Are you trying to kill your watch off?' He walked over to the station officer who was still being attended to by Fireman Burnett. 'You look like one of Clay's victims.' The chief officer was referring to the new young heavyweight Cassius Clay who appeared to be invincible. The station officer tried valiantly to explain the catalogue of disasters to Cutting but without a great deal of success, as the realisation, that during his frantic efforts to avoid the burning tyres he had lost his false teeth had not dawned on him.

'For God's sake, stop bashing your gums together and make some sense, man.'

Silvers strove to make another spirited attempt at an explanation, when the loss of his plate became embarrassingly obvious as he spat over the chief officer.

'When you've finally extinguished this little epic and dealt with the dead and wounded, report back to me at the station.' Cutting wiped his lapel with his sleeve. 'Oh, and try to find your bloody teeth as well.' The chief officer wandered back to his car, mumbling to himself, whilst trying to wipe the saliva from his undress jacket. We managed to put out the fire without further incident and then joined the station officer in trying to retrieve his choppers, but due to a mixture of smouldering lumps of molten rubber and other debris, the task proved fruitless. Silvers climbed back into the pump, holding a piece of lint against his eye, whilst Bert and Vic were helped painfully into the rear cab. The leading fireman informed the control that the pump was off the run due to our misfortune and drove back to the station.

'Cutting's going to need a raincoat in there,' quipped Jeff, nodding towards the station officer's office, as we sat down to a welcome cup of tea in the recreation room.

'I could murder a pint now,' Vic said, still gently rubbing his injured leg.

'Better not, the old man's not in the best of moods,' I replied. Fireman Evans explained that as he and Bert were now officially off the run for the remainder of the watch, there was no harm in opening up the bar. 'Besides, if he upsets me, he won't get these bleeders back.' Vic's pugnacious face beamed with delight as he held Silvers's ivories aloft. 'Anyway, they can't hang me now, they've just done away with the death sentence.' He tossed the false teeth high into the air and made a vain attempt to catch them as they clattered on to the snooker table.

Chapter Ten

Christmas 1964 was now fast approaching and once again the lottery to get it off was about to commence. After the draw for the drivers and specialists such as the ET and TL crews had been decided, the remainder of the names were drawn. There was no incentive to work at Christmas; the hourly rate was the normal basic, but if you worked, a day off in lieu could be claimed and as yet I hadn't had a Christmas off. (I wasn't to know that I wouldn't get one off for the next twelve years because of the changes of shifts I would encounter.)

'Hard luck, Hooligan, you lose all round, mate.' I took Vic's remark with a quizzical stare. 'Officer in charge cooks the Christmas dinner,' he continued pointing towards Bert Cross. The station officer had been on duty on the last occasion and had therefore elected to have this Christmas off.

'You can cook, Bert, can't you?' He looked at me and smiled.

"Course I can, boy, old army man, me, cook any bleedin' thing.' He plunged his hand down the inside of the front of his trousers and began to scratch with great gusto at his private parts. The whole watch burst into laughter at the stricken countenances of Ken, Dave and myself.

'Stuffing the chicken takes on a whole new concept of culinary skills when Bert does the cooking,' said Alan Cobb, placing a parodying arm of comfort on my shoulder. 'Tends to take the instructions literally,' he mused.

'Think I'll bring sandwiches in,' retorted Dave.

'Can't you come in?' implored Ken Smith of the cook.

'No way! Look on the bright side, though, you'll all be off with some dreadful disease for the New Year.' Her huge frame shook with laughter as she nudgingly winked at Bert.

The Christmas tour of duty went without much incident, save for one exception. We were called to a chimney fire in a row of flats, three storeys high with communal chimney stacks at either end of the building and in the middle. The occupier was, to say the least, full of festive spirit and persisted in telling us in no uncertain terms that he did not hold the fire service in great esteem, a fact that fell on deaf ears apart from one, the sub-officer. We had to drag Bert back into the passage to restrain him after the tenant had suggested that he was a wanker and in all probability not very good at that either. 'Useless lot of bastards,' he bellowed as the contents of the Watneys Red Barrel bottle in his hand spewed over the carpet. 'Piss off.' He pointed his arm downwards and then made a gigantic sweeping motion towards the street door as the beer cascaded down on us.

I pushed the irate tenant back into the living room whilst the rest of the PE crew tried to calm Bert down. 'You'll leave this place like a shitheap. I've heard all about you lot.' I looked around the room. It would be virtually impossible to make the place look more slovenly than this guy's efforts. There were the remains of some turkey bones scattered around the room and several unwashed dinner plates lying amid numerous empty cream label stout bottles. He'd taken care of them and was in the process of making a start on the Red Barrel bottles, when we had interrupted his binge. Large patches of grease had soaked into the carpet and chairs over several years of such indulgences.

'Come on, mate, you sit yourself down in the armchair while we put the fire out.'

'Piss off! I've only just lit the bastard, now you pricks want to put the bloody fing out.' I tried to explain that his chimney was alight and if not extinguished could spread to the other flats because of the age of the properties. 'Bollocks.' He paused briefly to burp in my face. 'Only damage likely is from you lotta tossers.' I assured him that we would put the fire out and leave his flat cleaner than it had ever been, which of course, was about as clever as saying that Hitler was a pacifist, bearing in mind the state of this guy. He grabbed my leather belt as he fell backwards into the armchair, pulling me down on top of him. Our faces were inches apart as the combined smell of the beer and his bad breath were belched into my face. 'Wot you sin sin sinuatin' you stuck up git?' I tried desperately to prise his fingers from my belt as he fell sideways out of the chair and on to the floor, dragging me with him.

'You all right, Hooligan?' Jeff helped pull me up. 'Now come on, mate, behave yourself, or we're going to have to call the police.' Jeff's threat seemed to work, as we lifted him back into the chair he adopted a very subdued attitude. The sub-officer had calmed down sufficiently to be allowed back into the room and take charge of operations, despite the scowling glare of the occupier and the occasional grunt of scorn as we proceeded to connect the bamboo chimney rods to the hose-reel.

'For Christ's sake, go easy with that stirrup pump, Daisy, we don't want sooty water all over the place.' Dave pushed down apprehensively as I poured more water into the galvanised bucket the pump stood in. 'How many rods on there now, Jeff?'

'About eight, Sub.'

'Sub! Wot's that for, sub bleedin' normal I s'pose,' the man in the chair scoffed.

'Take no notice, Bert,' I said worriedly, adding a further rod to the chimney gear. 'That makes nine, now.'

'We must be out the top by now,' Bert said, removing his helmet and scratching his head. 'Go and have a look outside, Smiffy.'

Ken went out into the street to see if the rods were protruding from the top of the pot. 'No sign of them yet, Sub, but there's still plenty of flame coming out.' Bert shook his head in disbelief and ordered Ken to get some more rods off the PE. We continued to screw the brass threads together, adding a further three rods as Daisy alternately pushed and pulled on the handle off the pump, whilst we carefully eased the rods and reel further up the chimney. Black sooty water was running back down the hose-reel and into the tiled hearth. I soaked the water up with a deck cloth and wrung it out into a spare bucket.

'The water's only lukewarm, Sub, it's not reaching the fire.'

'It must be,' Bert demanded. 'We've got enough rods on there to reach—' He stopped in mid-sentence. 'Oh shit! Anyone in next door, mate?'

The man grunted back, "E's on shifts, old woman's staying at 'er son's.'

Bert dashed out into the street pulling me with him as he ordered Daisy to stop pumping. He agitatedly banged the iron door knocker of the next-door flat. 'Come on, come on,' he urged. The man opened the door, dressed in a pair of large cotton underpants, tucked into his black woollen socks. He tried to pull his vest down to cover the large expanse of belly being displayed. He rubbed his eyes, disbelievingly at the sight before him.

'What's up? Am I on fire?'

The sub-officer pushed past the startled man as I made our apologies. 'Fucking 'ell!' The anguished cry from Bert must have been heard next door because the rest of the crew had now dashed into the passage. I peered over Bert's shoulder into the living room. There must have been about fifty feet of chimney rods and hose-reel curled around the room like a mass of entwined spaghetti. Black sooty water was running down the walls.

'I didn't realise I was alight,' the man said apologetically, as he surveyed the devastation.

'Are you going to tell him, or shall I?' whispered Jeff into my ear.

By now the guy from next door had staggered into the hallway and after his initial burst of laughter, took great delight in explaining to his neighbour the shortcomings of the fire service. 'I told yer, didn't I? Told yer they're a buncha wankers.' The sub-officer was too shocked to even retaliate to his jibes, which was just as well, really, because now a passing policeman had entered the already over-crowded passage. More neighbours were also trying to push their way through to view the havoc we had created.

Alan Cobb was the ideal man to pacify the distraught tenant. He placed a reassuring arm around the man and began to explain the intricacies of chimney construction in great detail. He rationalised that the metal inspection plate on his chimney breast had not been bolted back properly and therefore had burst open when the rods were forced into next door's flue. Alan's calm demeanour seemed to pacify the man to the extent that he appeared quite relieved that it was not his fault and that the council could take the rucking his wife would have surely given him upon her return. The PE crew had the task of dismantling the rods and cleaning up the sitting room as best they could whilst the leading fireman gave the occupier contact numbers within the council to claim for the damage inflicted. The pump's crew returned next door to finally extinguish the fire and clean up.

'I told yer, I told yer, didn't I?' The drunken tenant waved his finger, emphasising every gesture as he slumped back into his chair, only to raise his buttocks painfully to one side to pass wind. He contorted his face to repeat the manoeuvre, groaning slowly at his failure this time.

'Wouldn't you be better in the other room, mate?' I asked.

'This is my 'ouse and I'll sit where I bleedin' well like.'

Ken Smith and I elected to clean the hearth up as this was slightly upwind of the continuous explosions emitting from the direction of the chair, where, inevitably, Daisy had ended up.

'Oh my god.' Fireman Woods jumped up from his bending position as the aftermath of another gaseous eruption wafted across the room.

'I detect a delicate bouquet of pickled onion in with the Red Barrel there, Smithy, don't you?' I wiggled my nose, careful not to breathe in too deeply as Ken nodded his agreement.

'All right, Hooligan, you go over there, then,' demanded Daisy indignantly.

'Come on, Dave, the sooner we get cleared up, the sooner we're out,' smiled Ken.

We had made a magnificent job of the clean-up, so much so that the flat was positively gleaming and certainly a damned sight cleaner than when we first entered. I rang the last drops of sooty water from the deck cloth into the bucket with a degree of pride as Bert entered the room. 'There you are, chief, the lads have done you proud there.' He had hardly finished the sentence when the man leapt from the chair, grabbed the bucket and threw the contents over the sub-officer. Mayhem ensued as Dave and I rugby-tackled Bert to the floor to prevent a possible murder and the leading hand grabbed the tenant around the arms to stop a further attack on the sub. 'For Christ's sake, get him out, Jim,' he yelled as we dragged Bert kicking and screaming into the street.

Bert's falsetto voice shrieked above the roar of the train passing overhead the metal bridge, 'I'll kill the bastard, I will, I'll kill the bastard!' He head-butted the side panel of the pump as we continued to restrain him. We had been witness to Bert throwing tins up in the air and heading them, back at the station, in moments of boredom or when a full moon was out, but were not ready for this little outbreak. He continued to assault the fire engine as Vic rushed to our aid. Vic spun Bert round and slammed him back up against the pump.

'Oi, come on you,' he threatened, 'knock it off or I'll slap yer.'

The sub appeared to calm down at the thought of a right-hander from the ex-boxer, in spite of the latter's self-confessed limitations at the noble art. We managed to bundle Bert into the machine and made our way back to Plaistow.

★

Over the next few weeks we eagerly awaited the transfers that were inevitable, due to the formation of the Greater London Fire Brigade. Plaistow were to lose their emergency tender, Stratford, being designated Eastern Command, were to lose their foam tender, but gain a turntable ladder, control van, command lorry and two staff cars with a total manpower of sixty-nine as opposed to Plaistow's fifty-four. Stratford were also to have twenty general staff, two fire prevention and twenty-five control room operatives.

It was on one of my night shifts that Station Officer Silvers called me, Daisy and Alan Cobb into his office to inform us that in the near future we were being transferred

to F21 Stratford, as it was to be called after the takeover –
whoops, sorry, amalgamation.

'What's the matter with you, you miserable sod,' Joan
placed my dinner in front of me and sat down at the table. I
explained that I was going back to Stratford and would
inevitably miss Jeff, Vic and the boys, and that I was
apprehensive of the larger formation we would all find
ourselves in. 'You'll probably get your promotion a lot
quicker in a bigger set-up.' I nodded agreement. I hadn't
really thought much about the Leading Fireman's practical
exams, but now realised why the West Ham Brigade had
been promoting everybody who was qualified. The practi-
cals in London were bound to be more difficult.

'I'll make a start on the hall tomorrow, Joan,' I said ab-
sently, still turning the probabilities of a quick promotion
over in my mind. No chance I thought; I haven't got any
other qualifications apart from BA. I would certainly have
to become a driver to have any chance. I had been promis-
ing Joan to paint the hall for ages and had been taking some
stick from her because we had visited Kay and Gordon at
their new house in Thundersley and of course, Gordon had
decorated the whole bloody place in about a week. He also
had the advantage that he hadn't inherited a dog called
Bobo.

Peggy Magill and her family had lived a few doors down
from me in St James's Road, Stratford. I had known them
virtually all my life, through the war years, into my teens
and now into married life. She was a tall, thin woman with
pronounced bone structure, making her face appear square
and flat, especially as her nose was more akin to someone of
African origin. She had, like many others just after the war,
a household that was always overcrowded, with five kids,
including two sets of twins, one ageing father-in-law, a
lodger and various pets.

The Magills were the first family down our road to acquire a black and white television in the early Fifties, when on Sundays it would seem the entire population of St James's Road would pile into her dining room to watch a drama called *Little Red Monkey* and *What's My Line*. At one stage we even had the added bonus of colour viewing. This was, in fact, a piece of transparent plastic with three coloured bands: blue at the top, red in the middle and green at the bottom. This was clipped to the screen – great for shots of John Wayne on the prairie, but a bloody disaster for close-ups of poor old Gilbert Harding.

In retrospect I had many things to be grateful for to Peggy Magill. I think my fascination for the female breast probably began when, as a ten year old with my sidekick, Kenny Cox, we watched open-mouthed as Peggy breastfed the twins during one of the Sunday shows. I seem to remember being attacked by one of the other mothers as she grabbed our ears and forced our attention back to the telly, informing all and sundry that we were a couple of dirty little sods who had been spotted on previous occasions trying to get Barbara Barnard and Valerie Watkins to show us their knickers.

The one thing, however, that I couldn't be grateful for was Bobo. The Magills decided to emigrate, as many did, in the Sixties, to Australia. They had acquired a mongrel dog which the kids wanted to take to the Antipodes. Peggy had persuaded them that it would be better to leave it in England with somebody else and that Joan and I were the ideal adopted parents for Bobo. This proved to be a mistake of gargantuan magnitude. The poor dog was used to being surrounded by kids and never really settled with us, in spite of desperate attempts to make it happy. It was always trying to escape, and the final straw broke the day I finally got round to painting the passage. I had placed a scaffolding board across the stairwell and was precariously balanced with my tin of white paint on the board, stretching to reach the coving. I had wedged the street door open to disperse the smell and locked Bobo in the garden.

'Where's the girl, Jim?' Percy pushed past the street door looking for his granddaughter. I had hardly finished telling him that she was on her swing in the garden when the demented dog scrambled past me and up the stairs.

'Joan, get this bloody dog locked up,' I yelled as it scampered past me once again, this time taking the ladder securing the scaffolding board. The board clattered down the stairs, quickly followed by me and the two-gallon tin of paint. The dog shot out into the street, frantically followed by the screaming Joan.

'You stupid Irish sod, I told you to lock him in,' she bellowed, jumping over me as I rolled into the passage, covered in paint. I lay there, wondering why I was always Irish when something like this happened and presumably English when I tended to avoid the odd disaster. I was still on my knees, struggling to get up when the street door was violently smashed against my head by the returning dog, who then dashed through spilt paint and up the stairs. I groggily started to close the door to prevent a further escape attempt by the mutt only to have the door impacted into my head once again by the frenzied entrance of my lady wife. 'Stupid Irish bastard!' I sat on the floor, rubbing my throbbing head, reflecting that there must be somewhere in this great country of ours where a bloody Englishman had the same misfortune as myself. The dog was now once again descending the stairs with Joan in hot pursuit. The white gloss paw and slipper prints were beginning to form quite a pretty pattern on the red fitted carpet as I managed to slam the street door shut. 'Get him, Dad,' Joan yelled as the dog scurried through the passage and into the garden. Still dazed from the assault by the hardwood door, I staggered out into the back yard, where Percy had managed to grab the paint-splattered Bobo by the neck. I would have been more selective and gone for the balls, but at least we had captured the little bugger. Corinne was ordered to stay on her swing, but seemed to appreciate the lighter side of the scenario before her as she burst into raptures of laughter at our attempts to restrain the slippery animal.

Bobo was eventually cleaned up and after much soul-searching taken to the vet where it was explained to us that it would have been kinder to put the animal to sleep when the Magills left for Australia. As it was now, finding a new home would prove difficult as he needed lots of attention, especially by children, and far more space than we had. Hopefully, he found that home.

Chapter Eleven

I grabbed the hot metal rail and pulled myself painfully forward once more. My black cork helmet fell over my eyes once again. Bloody thing! I wrenched at the studded leather strap and threw the helmet into the oily black sludge under the metal causeway. 'You all right, Hooligan?' grunted Jeff, turning on his stomach. He had gained quite a distance between us in the prop-shaft tunnel. The ebbing beam from his CEAG lamp highlighted my helmet floating in the morass of stagnant water and oil. I managed to force some sort of acknowledgement from my aching carcass as I dug my elbows into the rough metal ribs of the floor, pushed the breathing bag in front of me once more and painfully edged forward another couple of feet. Jesus, I'm probably going to die in this shit hole. I don't believe it! I've got my bloody leggings caught up now. I pulled frantically at the leggings, ripping them in the process. Surely God, you must owe me a couple of favours; didn't I serve as an altar boy at St Francis? I learnt the catechism; look, I'll prove it. Who made you? God made me. Why did God make you? God made me to love him and serve him. In whose image did God make you? Image, image – what's that? I knew it couldn't be Jeff's torch; it was too bright.

'Jeff.'

'Yeah, I can see it, Jim.' Jeff forgot about the height restriction as he tried to raise himself off the floor. 'Bollocks.' His helmet clattered to the floor, rolling into the mire.

'Down here, down here,' I yelled at the beam as it jogged towards us.

'Is that you, O'Halloran?' The soft Scottish accent of Jim Docherty was pure music. Stratford's crew had been ordered to make their way down the prop-shaft from the tunnel entrance and had got about a quarter of the way along when they found us. 'You two are a pain in the arse. We've got to reverse back up now.' Sub-Officer Docherty wasn't wearing BA as all the sets were in full use, and had obviously volunteered himself and some other poor unfortunate bugger as a rescue crew. He had a delightful habit of doing this with his men. His reasoning was that if an 'old' man like him could do it, then you must be able to. It worked extremely well, as no one wanted to be shown up.

We scrambled up on to the Jacob's ladder, through the store and out of the door at the side of the ship's funnel, into the cold morning air and the vista of the Silvertown skyline. I never thought East 16 could look so wonderful. Even the pungent mixture of odours from Tate and Lyle and Knight's soap factory were comparable to some exotic elixir. I stood on deck for a few moments, my mouthpiece ripped aside, as I gulped in large chunks of air. Jeff was on his knees, totally exhausted, covered in black greasy oil from head to toe.

'Where's your helmet, old O'Halloran?' I stared at Silvers in total disbelief. I looked anxiously at the deformed mouth for traces of a faint smile, but there were none. He was deadly serious. 'Have you lost yours as well old Burnett?'

'For Christ's sake Sid, piss off, leave them alone.' The large frame of Docherty loomed over Silvers grabbing his arm and pulling him aside. 'Are you all right, Jim?' I nodded, still in a state of shock from my experience. Jeff was still on his knees, being comforted by Vic who appeared almost as distressed as us at our dishevelled state.

'Do you want an ambulance?' Jeff shook his head vigorously as Vic assisted him to his feet. He turned slowly towards me, shaking his head as if trying to explain his innermost feelings of relief, joy, and the fact that the continuous encouragement we had given each other had bonded our comradeship even more. He lifted his oil-splattered arm above his head and slapped his hand across my outstretched palm. 'Well done, Hooligan.'

'Come on you two, let's get you back to the station.' Bert put his arm around my shoulder as we made our way on to the swaying gangplank and down to the dockside.

After breakfast I went to the dormitory and cleaned my gear up. Alan Cobb was ruefully removing a photograph of a particularly well-endowed nude model which he had taken at one of his photographic clubs. 'Sorted out your helmet and leggings yet, Jim?'

'That little bastard had the audacity to say that he wouldn't press charges this time,' I replied, referring to the dressing down I had just received from Silvers.

'We're well rid of him, mate, he's just had another go at Vic about his log bookings.'

Alan had hardly finished the sentence when we heard Bert shouting at Vic in the appliance bay. 'Don't be bloody stupid, Vic, you'll only come unstuck, son.'

Alan and I rushed into the appliance bay and were confronted by Silvers being gripped tightly round the throat and dragged back towards his own office by Fireman Evans. 'Come on *old* Silvers, you and me 'ave got to sort out a few ground rules before the next shift.' Vic bundled the station officer into the office and slammed the door behind him.

'I wouldn't interfere if I were you, Jim.' Alan pulled my arm sharply as I tried to enter Silvers's office. He was right of course, the persistent victimisation of the younger elements of the watch and in particular Fireman Evans, was bound to come to a head at some stage, and this was it.

'I'm warning you, old Evans.' Silvers's protestations were abruptly halted as Vic pushed him into his chair. We got closer to the door, trying to peer through the curtain covering the half-glass in the top of the door.

'Shut up and listen.' Vic proceeded to lay down terms and conditions that were to apply to any future encounters between himself, Silvers and the rest of the watch. He continued for some time, without interruption from the station officer and finally emerged from the office with a satisfied grin on his lived-in features. 'Don't fink we'll be 'aving any problems from that little shit for a while.' He marched purposefully back to the watch room and shut the door.

'Pity you're leaving, it could be very interesting here,' smiled Bert as we made our way back to the dormitory to continue cleaning our gear.

Alan glanced wistfully at his latest photograph before attempting to place it in a large blue folder with his other works of art. 'Has this one got big tits, Alan?' He peered above his reading glasses and disdainfully thrust the picture into my hand.

'I thought you were a bit different from the other morons, Hooligan; I'm obviously going to have to educate you about the finer aspects of photography.' He had scarcely finished admonishing me when Jeff attempted to lean over my shoulder.

'More tits, Cobby?'

'Christ, I expected you to be more objective, Jeff.'

Fireman Burnett, who was a keen photographer himself, took the picture from me. He studied it carefully for a while, scratching his mop of wavy black hair, and then handed it back to me. 'What do you reckon, Jim?'

'We're getting worried about you, Al,' I replied, rotating the photo in my hands. 'It's a rusty nut and bolt on a farm gate, taken after a rainstorm,' replied Alan.

Alan grabbed the photograph from my hands and stuffed it into the folder.

'We knew what it was, Alan, that's why we're worried about you.'

Alan Cobb had suggested that I take my old Kodak camera to work on the next shift and he would instruct me on the basics of taking a good photograph. During the lunch break Alan drove the TL into the yard, downed the jacks and pitched the hundred foot Merryweather ladder to its full working height. Under Alan's expertise and guidance, I took numerous shots, both at ground level and from the top of the ladder. I was really beginning to appreciate terms like 'depth of field' and 'framing' a short when once again the call bells beckoned me to yet another rubbish fire on the Munday Road estate. As I clambered on to the pump I thrust the camera into Vic's hands. 'Look after that for me 'till I get back.' Fireman Evans smiled as he pulled the rope to open the large wooden appliance room doors and waved us on our way.

I gave no thought to this mundane incident until I returned home to Dersingham Avenue about three weeks later after finishing a quiet day shift. My mother-in-law, Amy, was sitting in the armchair with Corinne on her lap gently humming to our daughter. I was just about to stoop down to kiss Corinne when Joan grabbed my arm forcefully and pulled me through the dining room door into the kitchen. 'In here, you! I want a bloody word with you.'

'Christ, you're ripping my shirt! What's the matter with you?'

'This!' She waved the tiny transparency from Kodak menacingly under my nose.

'Your films came back today, and Mum opened them.'

'So?' I replied, innocently.

'Thank Christ she didn't have her glasses with her,' Joan continued, poking me in the chest with the transparency.

'They're only shots of the TL; what's the problem?' I continued, trying to avoid the sharp jabs into my chest. 'She was holding this one up to the light and asking if I'd put on bloody weight!' I wrestled the film from Joan's grasp and held it up to the kitchen light.

'Bastards!' I blinked to clear my vision in case I was mistaken. No! there was no mistake. I thought to myself: I can name every one of those bare arses from left to right. It took a lot of persuasion on my part to convince Joan that Evans and Co had 'enhanced' my collection of fire brigade memorabilia with their own artistic interpretation of photography.

★

'You still reading that bleedin' book, Woodsie?' Vic pulled his locker door open as Daisy turned another page of the huge manuscript. 'Must be bloody interesting!' Dave raised his head and gave a superior nod of agreement.

Jeff burst through the locker room door. 'It's pissing down out there!'

'That's very observant Jeffrey, it's been raining for the past four bloody days; where have you been for God's sake?' I asked.

'Fishing,' he retorted. 'Didn't notice it really.'

'It's flooded down by the docks,' Vic said, buckling his black leather belt around his fire tunic ready for roll call. I rubbed the toes of my shoes on to the back of my woollen fire trousers to buff them up a bit. 'Try polishing them, Hooligan,' I shrugged my shoulders negatively as the bells sounded for change of watch. Vic glanced over Daisy's shoulder as he rose to go out. 'Page 402! 'Ow many pages in that soddin' book?'

'Just over five hundred,' replied Dave arrogantly.

'*Daily* fuckin' *Mirror*'s got too many for me!' retorted Vic. I'd noticed that Vic was developing an amazing ability to dissect certain nouns with Anglo-Saxon adjectives. He'd recently informed us that one of his mates had moved to Billerfuckin'ricay in Essex.

Bert read the list of riders for the watch. 'White watch present and correct, sir.' The sub-officer was just about to dismiss the roll call, when the station officer interjected.

'Just a minute, old Sub.' A distorted smile akin to that of a bondage freak in a leather factory oozed from Silvers's lips.

'Your belt line Evans?'

'Yes, Guv?' a puzzled Vic replied.

'Cleaned it lately?'

'Yes, Guv,' I glanced at Vic's self-rescue line attached to his axe belt. It was Daz-white, bloody gleaming!

'Impressed are you, old O'Halloran?' sneered Silvers. 'Well don't be. Take it off, old Evans.' Vic undid the large chrome buckle and slid the belt line off. 'Undo it, then.' As it took some considerable time to form the fifteen foot piece of rope into the required configuration, Vic was not at all pleased. He handed the line to the station officer, who dangled it from his right hand triumphantly. 'Fireman Evans has been cleaning this without undoing it. Note the black bits in between the white bits; looks like a bleedin' zebra crossing,' he whined. 'He's also been cleaning it with Omo and bleach, haven't you, old Evans.' Vic acknowledged by shrugging his shoulders. 'Now, if Fireman Evans were to find himself dangling from this belt line, with the flames licking 'round his arse, he'd probably break his fucking neck. It's totally buggered!' he bellowed into Vic's ear. 'I don't want to see anyone with a line like that. Clean them and dry them properly before you make them up,' he screamed at the watch.

'The rest of the watch can have a make and mend at three o'clock, Sub,' he continued quite deliberately, his face twisting into a smirk, 'except old Evans. He can do the weekly checks on the machines.' Vic would be working until 5.30, whilst we were stood down.

Bert continued with the roll call. 'White watch, for your duties, fall out.' Silvers seemed to include a couple of light skips into his stride as he made his way to the office. And so another day's duty was about to begin. Bob Annis was just pouring the tea when the bells went down. He hurriedly tipped the cups back into the brown enamel pot and left it to stew on the gas ring.

'That'll be nice when we get back,' said Smithy sarcastically.

'Road flooded down by Harlands, didn't give the name,' shouted Alan Cobb as he passed the call slips he had just scrawled out to the officers in charge of the pump and pump escape.

'That's Silly-bleedin'-town's ground,' shouted Vic as he plunged his arms into his fire tunic.

'Could be East Ham's,' retorted Bert from the front passenger's seat. 'They must all be out.'

We sped south down Prince Regent's Lane and turned left at the bottom towards numbers 8 and 9 gates of the Royal Docks. 'Poxy swing bridge is open, throw a left into 9 gate, we'll go along the KG5 dockside.' The huge ship *American Star* was making its way painstakingly through the narrow channel into the Royal Victoria Dock. The queue of traffic would be there for some considerable time.

'Jesus, Vic,' cried Bert as Fireman Evans swerved firstly to miss the massive wheeled crane as it trundled along the quayside and then to miss a gang of dockies huddled beside a huge net filled with bales of cargo. I glanced back at the shocked group who were gesticulating with some fierce animation, which suggested that Vic was not driving, but masturbating. 'Ker-fuckinf-meedians,' Vic mumbled as we flashed past the berthed ships, Bert frantically ringing the large chrome bell, whilst leaning towards the dashboard to flash the headlights. The sub-officer drew his knees up towards his chin and let out a loud high-pitched shrill, closing his eyes as Vic managed to squeeze the PE between one of the crane wheels and a trolley left unattended on the dockside. I turned round and looked out of the window as the trolley majestically did three pirouettes before slowly tumbling into the dock. Vic was in enough trouble with the old man, and as nobody else seemed to notice, I ignored the incident. We turned out of the dock gate and bumped across the railway lines that straddled the cobbled road between the KG5 dock and Gallions Reach and turned left into a small dead-end road of red-brick terraced houses. The water was knee-deep but as yet had not breached the stone steps of the houses.

As I jumped out of the PE, the water gushed up between my black 'waterproof' leggings and my knee-high leather boots, filling them almost instantaneously. 'Oh shit.' Bert had obviously filled his boots too. We waded towards the end of the road and peered over the wall which was supposed to be holding the Thames back. The debris in the river rushed past us, clattering into wooden mooring posts as the deafening crescendo cascaded around the bend towards Gallions Reach.

'What's the problem, Bert?' shouted Silvers, who had maintained his position at the front of the pump.

'Can't do a lot 'ere, Guv, we'd just be pumping it back up the hill, waste of bloody time.'

The station officer picked up his phone and ordered the station's allocation of sandbags to be delivered for the residents. 'You might as well go back, Sub, with your crew, no point in tying two machines up here.'

We started to drag our increasingly heavy boots back towards the pump escape.

'Oi! Ain't yer goin' ter do anyfing, mate.' The gentleman standing at his street door in shirt and braces with trousers rolled up to the knees only needed a knotted handkerchief and he would have been togged out for Southend.

Bert leant against the PE's door slowly pulling his right boot off, which in turn wrenched his sock from his foot and emptied what must have been ten pints back into the brown swirling water. He raised his head slowly, looked towards the tenant and said, 'You will observe, sir, that I have been walking through the water, not sodding well on it!' He slammed the door shut as we made our way back through the dockside and past a bewildered dockie who was trying to explain to his ganger that his trolley had been there before he went for a piss. The incessant scratching of his mates' heads assured me that no one had seen Vic's genteel nudge.

We pulled into the yard and whilst Bert booked us back we checked to see if the collision had marked the appliance. It looked fine except for one small mark where the red paint had scratched off on the driver's door. 'Shit, we'll have to touch it up before the old man gets back.'

Jeff placed his hand on Vic's shoulder. 'Don't worry, mate, I've got just the thing for that.' He disappeared into the store and emerged with a thin piece of red plastic which was identical to the colour of the fire engine. 'Wet that, mate,' he said, licking the tiny piece of cellophane-like substance, 'and Bob's your uncle.' He slapped it over the offending mark. It was miraculous; you really couldn't spot it.

'What if it falls off later?' enquired Vic.

'Not our bloody problem, mate, is it?'

Over the next few shifts, that piece of red plastic must have fallen off dozens of times, and each time the station officer discovered with some relish that he had found a scratch, he was instantly convinced that he was seeing things, as the piece of cellophane was quickly stuck over it. He was too vain to produce his reading glasses in front of the lads. Even the sub-officer played along for a while. Silvers didn't find it at all amusing when he finally discovered the deception. We would undoubtedly pay for it later.

On my days off, I had decided to do some more 'diamonds' as a means of earning a few more shillings. My father-in-law, Percy, had a thirty foot wooden extension ladder and had made a wooden box barrow with some old pram wheels to which to attach the ladder and bucket. We had decided that the best place for window cleaning would be Goodmayes, as we already had captive customers there: my mother and my grandparents, along with their neighbours and friends in the vicinity. Most of the houses were large double-fronted semis with concrete window sills surrounding the bay windows. Percy would clean the bottoms whilst I did the tops. The sills were wonderful because once I had climbed the ladder to the first floor, I could then virtually walk from house to house without getting back on the ladder. In retrospect, I must have been utterly insane. If one of those old sills had broken, I could have been seriously injured. I could even have lost my job or, even worse, been killed. The crazy thing is, I would never have taken that chance in the fire brigade. We just did one day each week.

On one of the days when, I wasn't doing the George Formby bit, the White Watch had decided to arrange a 'friendly' game of football on Wanstead Flats against the Port of London Authority Police. This was to prove a bad error of judgement on the organiser's part, one Paddy McGinty. We assembled at a well-known area of what is part of Epping Forest locally known as the Sand Hills – a few mounds of sandy dirt skirting a lake with an island in its centre. The football pitches had a few uneven mounds themselves.

'Bloody changing rooms are miles away, I'm toggin' out 'ere,' said Vic. Bert didn't fancy the hike either and proceeded to strip off, making no conscious effort to save the local residents of Wanstead a full-frontal bombardment.

'You should wear a jockstrap, Paddy, they're hard bastards,' said Tom Delarue, who looked as elegant as ever, his hair looking as though it had just been hot-tonged into rows of sickly black waves. 'It's a friendly, they just want a run out to keep fit.' The police played in the Thursday afternoon business league, where the will to win was such that it was not unknown for some of the teams to play 'ringers' who looked remarkably like some of the up-and-coming young professionals we saw on occasional Saturdays at the Boleyn. We were just about ready to take to the pitch when the PLA police team ran out from the old tin hut that was the changing room.

'Jesus Christ! Have you seen the size of those bastards, Jeff?' Jeff turned away from me and was visibly shaken when he saw the tribe of Neanderthal men trundling towards us.

'Think I'll go home now,' said Daisy, the blood draining slowly from his face. Smithy was trying to say something to allay our fears but to no avail. It was down to Paddy, our revered captain, to suppress our state of total panic. 'I fink we're gonna die.'

'Don't be bloody stupid,' retorted Bert, his hand stuffed down the front of his shorts, scratching his wedding tackle. 'One good kick in the bollocks, that'll slow 'em down.'

'I think you'd better keep your hand down there Bert, yours could end up round your ears.' He scoffed at my remark, pulled the woollen khaki hat over his head and ran on to the pitch.

'Is he wearing that bloody thing?' queried Tom. 'They'll think we're a right bunch of prats.'

Tom started to go through a most amazing routine of warming up exercises; whether this was to persuade the other side that we were all about or not, I'm not so sure, but it certainly drained Tom of any energy he may have possessed.

'I've a funny feeling I'm going to get severe backache this afternoon,' drawled Alan Cobb, our goalkeeper, 'picking the bloody ball out of the net.' I had seen Alan perform in the five-a-side kickabouts at the station, and in spite of his age he had obviously been quite useful in his younger days. His craggy countenance never seemed to change, no matter what mood he was in.

I had been picked as centre half; heaven knows why, as at five foot ten I would most certainly be struggling against their centre forward, who dwarfed me not only by a good eight inches, but also by a considerable weight advantage. 'Shit, I think I'm going to get seriously hurt here, Paddy.'

'You'll be all right, son, you've got youth on your side.' And not much else, I thought to myself as I looked around the dishevelled bunch of sacrificial offerings who were my team mates.

'Good afternoon, I've come to cause you a little bit of bother.' I stared at the centre forward I was about to mark when the framed silhouette, blocking the sun's rays, grabbed my hand and shook it vigorously. I half expected my hand to be crushed, but was pleasantly surprised to feel no semblance of pain; in fact, it was quite a limp handshake.

I stupidly persuaded myself that I was probably marking the only six foot six poof in the PLA Police.

The referee, an 'impartial' retired policeman, or so they told us, gave a shrill blast on his whistle to commence the game. Directly from the kick-off a huge 'Garryowen' up-and-under ball was lifted skywards towards our goal. The ball probably had ice on it as it hurtled down towards us.

'I've got it, Al.'

'No, it's all right, Hooligan, I've got it.' I remember a feeling of being raised bodily as if in slow motion, and performing a triple somersault an Olympic diver would have won medals for. My shoulders crunched into the ground with a shuddering force jarring my back. I lay there for what seemed an eternity, trying to gasp some air into my deflated lungs. The birds had stopped singing and the boots with their hooped socks were silently gliding past me. I rolled slowly over on to my back. The pounding sound of studded football boots was gradually becoming louder as I mistakenly thought the worst was over. I peered into the sunlight, shading my eyes only to see the stricken green-jerseyed body of Alan Cobb hurtling towards me. I tried frantically to raise my aching body up but the ensuing collision was inevitable. I swear I sank a further two feet into the ground as Cobby landed directly on top of me. I rolled Alan's limp body off mine as the 'poof' gleefully grabbed the leather-laced ball from out the back of our net.

'No, you're both wrong, it was my ball,' he chortled, stepping over us as he made his way back to the centre circle. Bob Annis frenziedly splashed the magic sponge over us as we lay groaning on the ground.

'You okay, boys?' I took a large gasp of air into my lungs and nodded that I was on the way to recovery. Alan slowly raised himself on to his knees. 'Jesus Christ! What was that?'

McGinty was remonstrating furiously with the referee for a foul but he was being totally ignored. Bob Annis gingerly helped Alan to his feet and it was obvious from the way he was holding his shoulder that he would be unable to remain the custodian of our goal.

Vic pulled the green knitted roll-neck jumper over his flattened nose and loosened his shoulders by going through a sparring routine. 'When I shout "leave it", O'Halloran, you fucking well leave it!' From the authoritative tone of his voice, I wasn't about to argue with him. After a further ten minutes' play we were another goal down from a very dubious offside position. Paddy and Bert chased the referee back to the centre circle and in their anxiety to attract his attention to the frantically-waving linesman, managed to trip him up.

At this point, I was naive enough to believe that what was to follow was purely accidental, with no previous forethought of malicious wounding. Paddy 'helped' the referee up by grabbing his arm and wrenching him up off the floor with such force it was a wonder his arm remained in its socket. They then forgot about their protestations and apologised profusely for any pain they had caused. The middle-aged man was in such discomfort, especially from the first-aid treatment being given by these two Samaritans, that he took no further part in the game. As both the linesmen were policemen, it was suggested by Vic and McGinty that an impartial official be selected from the puzzled onlookers. A thick-set man with greying hair was reluctantly persuaded to take on the onerous responsibility of the whistle. He most certainly appeared to be a person not to argue with and assured everyone he had nothing to do with the Old Bill or the Fire Brigade. He tucked his socks into his jeans, adjusted the thick canvas braces and belt covering his more than adequate stomach and gave a shrill blast on the whistle to recommence battle.

By half-time we were three nil down, with Smithy and Daisy nursing bleeding noses from the havoc the centre forward and his minders were causing. Tom Delarue had also suffered some kind of injury, but nobody appeared to take much notice of his pain and suffering. After being tackled, he had rolled over so many times, he managed to end up on the sideline and had then proceeded to crawl on all fours from the halfway line around the perimeter of the pitch to the goal, where he dramatically made several valiant attempts to pull himself up via the goal post before collapsing in a heap.

'Isn't anyone going to help him?' I asked.

'Take no notice of the prat, he always does that,' said Gordon Bliss.

We started the second half with an exact replica of the first few minutes, when a high ball was lofted into our goal area. I reluctantly ran towards the effigy of Primo Carnera bearing down on me. My bravery could be summed up in two words: 'Fucking Stupid'.

'Mine, Hooligan,' screamed Vic as he sprinted off his goal line. I swerved out of the way to leave Fireman Evans to his fate. The ensuing goalkeeper's punch Vic was about to misdirect in the general direction of the ball was most certainly not out of the Upton Park Academy of Football's manual, more the Marquis of Queensbury's. The straight-arm clearance was replaced by a very orthodox-looking right uppercut that started from below his waist and travelled with the utmost ferocity, taking the shortest route to the constable's granite-like chin. The sickening impact of flesh and bone echoed around the ground as the police-man's body thudded into the ground. He was totally motionless. 'Referee!' screamed the milling policemen as they gathered threateningly around the newly appointed official.

'You all right, goalie?' he enquired, as Vic shook his swelling knuckles vigorously.

'Sod him! What about him?' shrieked their captain, pointing to the stationary body on the ground.

'It was a fair challenge. They both went for the ball,' replied the referee. 'In fact; your guy impeded the goalkeeper, you're lucky I didn't give a foul.' The staring, open-mouthed countenance of their skipper, at this reply, was a joy to behold. There were several more encounters of overzealous tackling and some very iffy offside decisions that all appeared to go in our favour, so much so that the match ended in a draw.

As the final whistle blew, I grabbed the hand of the still-bewildered centre forward who hadn't a clue what day of the week it was. 'Nice one, mate.' He pulled the blood-stained sponge away from his mouth and tried to mumble a reply. I think he was trying to say 'bollocks', but only succeeded in doing a fair impression of a ventriloquist talking whilst drinking water.

'How's the hand, Vic?' Jeff lifted Vic's swollen hand up. 'Looks worse than it is, mate,' replied the ex-boxer. I glanced over Jeff's shoulder to see the referee hurrying towards his Ford Zephyr to make a quick getaway.

'He was blinding, that ref,' said Smithy excitedly.

'Yeah, good bloke, old Dickie,' replied Paddy McGinty. I stopped in my tracks.

'You know him?'

Paddy smiled. ''Es an old mucker of mine, 'ates bleedin' rozzers, did about eight years for armed robbery. Well pleased with today's result.'

Over the next few weeks, every entry and exit into the docks by a fire engine bearing the West Ham coat of arms was subjected to the most rigorous search at the gates. Bad losers, the Old Bill!

Chapter Twelve

The wind gusted past my frozen face as the full vista of Prince Regent Lane and the surrounding area came into view from the top of the hundred foot Merryweather turntable ladder. Alan, who was operating it from the metal seat at the bottom, leaned over to the communication box. 'You're sure you're hooked on, Hooligan?' I glanced down towards my waist and tugged at the steel snap hook that hung from the leather belt. I assured myself it was firmly fixed to the steel ring attached to the top of the ladder. I leant forward to the voice amplifier.

'Yeah, okay, Al.'

'Keep your toes clear, I'm going to pawl the ladder.' I shuffled my feet backwards, making sure Alan could see the heels of my shoes protruding from the levered platform at the top of the ladder. I heard the metal click of the pawl as it cleared the rounds and then waited for Fireman Cobb to slowly lower the ladder a few inches to allow the pawl to lock on to the round. 'Okay, Jim, I'm just going to rotate the platform and lower the ladder over the back of the chassis, hold on.' The rest of the watch were down below on the drill yard, running lengths of hose out on to an imaginary fire in the drill tower. The ladder jerked slightly as the hydraulic system was engaged. Alan pushed his right knee against the protruding bar on the consul and the ladder began to slowly rotate in a clockwise direction. All rotary movements were done with the operator's legs, whilst two hand-operated levers controlled the elevation and depression of the ladder. By now Alan had turned the ladder through one hundred and eighty degrees and had started to slowly depress the ladder over the rear of the fire engine. 'Don't panic if the jacks move slightly; it's all part of the safety procedure.' I wasn't unduly worried by Cobby's remark as I couldn't even see the screwed jacks from my position. The ladder was probably extended to about eighty feet, twenty feet short of its maximum, and therefore the manoeuvre Alan was performing had a safety cut out to prevent the ladder from toppling over. As the ladder was further depressed I found it difficult to stand up right and was slowly falling forward with the front of my body pressed against the rounds. 'Right, that'll do,' said Alan as he stopped all movements. By now I was staring down into the drill yard with nothing between the top of the ladder and me, save sixty odd feet of freezing cold space. I glanced over my shoulder, stretching my neck to see where the chassis was. I had been in this position many times before and was always in awe of the incredible perspective below. As you peered down the side of the ladder, the steel reinforced hand rail disappeared down into what now looked like a Dinky toy fire engine and the same thought I always got at this sight was here again. How on earth was all this unsupported weight controlled by just hydraulic fluid? Amazing! Whilst I was lost in wonderment, I failed to realise what was going on below me. Alan had vacated the only controls of the ladder and wandered off to a place of safety. I gazed down in the resigned knowledge that I was about to get very wet. It was no good unhooking myself and trying to climb down, as the force of the jets would knock me off the ladder. I buried my helmet into the rounds and waited for the inevitable avalanche of freezing cold water that was about to hit me. No wonder Smithy and Daisy stepped aside when Bert had asked who wanted to ride the TL. Like a prat, I had volunteered for this with prompting from my so-called friends, Vic and Jeff. The deluge cascaded over me, the sheer volume soaking through my fire gear within seconds. It seemed to go on for ever until Silvers emerged from his office and stormed into the yard.

'What are you sodding about for old O'Halloran? You're supposed to be learning the onerous duties of a TL rider, not looking like a passenger off the Titanic. Get the idiot down, old Cobby.' Alan grinned as he mounted the consul and proceeded to bring me down to ground level. 'And get this gear made up before smoke-o.' The station officer strode off towards the mess room. I unhooked myself from the O-ring and climbed down off the TL. We started to hoist the hemp hose up the drill tower to drain and dry out when the bells went down. I clambered on to the back of the pump, my boots squelching from the water still contained in them.

'Jesus! I'm bloody frozen!' I wrapped my arms around my sodden fire tunic in a vain attempt to squeeze some warmth into my body. 'Wait till I get those two bastards on the ET.' Jeff and Vic were leering out of the window from the rear double doors of the swaying emergency tender as we chased it towards Plaistow tube station.

'RTA. Upper Road, persons trapped, get the first-aid box ready,' shouted Silvers. We turned off just before the station and pulled up on the bridge that crossed the Northern Outfall sewer. A Bedford van had smashed into a lamp post, ripping it from its base, and carried it six feet before smashing it into the metal railings of the bridge. The front of the van had taken most of the impact and it was apparent that the engine had been shunted back into the driver's compartment, crushing and collapsing the steering column. Smithy grabbed the steel-shod lever off the pump and started to prise the crumpled driver's door open, whilst the ET crew struggled to get the oxyacetylene cutting gear off. I stood behind Smithy with the first-aid box as he cursed his way through his task. The door suddenly sprang open with a loud crack as the lock mechanism gave way under the force being applied. Bert had already got into the passenger's side and was holding the driver's bloody chin, gently moving his head at the same time.

'You're all right, mate, soon have you out, don't worry.' His legs were not visible but were obviously trapped under the tangled mass of metal. Dave went to the front of the van and with the help of the leading fireman managed to force the battered bonnet open. 'Cut the positive battery lead, Daisy, there's petrol pissing out all over the place under here.' 'Start washing the petrol away from the van someone' yelled Silvers.

Dave snapped the huge bolt-croppers through the lead to kill the electrics, then reeled back in horror. 'Bloody hell, there's a kid under this lot!'

Silvers dived under the front wheels, 'Quick, get a jack over here,' he screamed at Bob Annis.

'Where do you want the cutting gear,' panted Jeff.

'Up here,' shouted Bert.

I continued rendering first-aid as best I could to the driver and was in the process of trying to feel the extent of the injuries to his legs when I pulled my hand away quickly. I screwed my face up in astonishment at the gooey mess on my blood-covered hand. 'Oh Jesus, he's puked up.' I quickly wiped my hand down the back of Bert's tunic.

'Fuck off, you Irish bastard.'

The sub stopped suddenly and twitched his nose. 'That's booze! This bastard's three sheets to the wind.'

'Let's get in there, Jim,' said Vic, pulling me aside, as he and Jeff ignited the cutting gear. 'Give the others a hand down there.'

'Go easy on that jack,' yelled Bert, 'don't forget we're in here.'

'I'll get the other first-aid gear off the ET,' I said.

Silvers looked up from his kneeling position. 'No need, son, she's dead.' Dave and the leading hand slumped back on their haunches, their faces contorted into a mixture of anger and frustration. 'We can't wait for the law if we want to get him out.' Silvers gestured towards the driver. 'Just jack it up gently and pull her out.' As the front axle cleared Daisy and I gingerly eased the limp body out and carried it away from the wreckage. We laid her on a salvage sheet and Dave gently placed his fire tunic over the upper part of her body whilst I covered her legs with mine. I would guess she was about eight or nine. I knelt down beside her and soothingly lifted the tiny hand protruding from under the tunic. I held it in the palm of my hand and gazed at the tiny fingers for a fleeting moment. They'd never be held by a boyfriend or lover, never be squeezed as she walked down a lane, never have rings on—

'Oi, come on, we've got to hose the engine down and wash the petrol away before they start cutting.' Bob pushed my helmet forward over my head. 'The ambulance is here now, anyway, they'll look after her.'

The ambulance man patted my back as if to console me as I made my way back to the van. I grabbed hold of the large fog applicator and began spraying a fine water mist over the engine as Jeff and Vic began burning through the twisted wreckage. Dave and Bob took two hose-reels and began diluting the petrol as they washed it into the gutter.

'Put some sand around the drain, old Smithy, stop it getting in to the sewers.' Silvers poked his head into the van. 'How's it going boys?'

'Can't really see too much down here, Guv, it's a right bloody mess,' replied Jeff. 'There's nowhere to put the blanket, can't get it between his leg and the steering column.' Vic pulled the asbestos blanket out once more and tried to readjust it to protect the driver's legs from the searing heat of the oxyacetylene torch.

'I wouldn't bother. Burn the bastard's legs off.'

Silvers glanced over towards the irate sub-officer. 'Okay, Bert, calm down, we're all a bit pissed off with this one; we've still got a job to do.'

Jeff and Vic tried to pacify Bert as he quickly wound himself up into a state of near-hysteria. 'Just leave us alone, Bert, go and head-butt the railings or something,' Jeff said angrily. As I pulled the sub-officer away from the van I did a double take on the driver's bloodstained countenance.

'That's the geezer who knocked me off my bloody bike!'

Bert spun round and wrenched himself from my grip, 'I'll kill the bastard!' Some puzzled bystanders watched in amazement as I wrestled Bert to the ground with the help of Smithy and Daisy.

'For Christ's sake, Bert, we're being watched.' I sat on his chest and pinned his arms above his head as the glazed mist appeared to envelope his eyes in a haze of vengeance. 'It's all right, Bert, take it easy, it's not our problem, let the rozzers sort it out.' I eased my grip as he rose slowly from the pavement, his teeth clenched tightly shut against his protruding jaw.

'I'm okay, just leave me.' He pushed his way past me and grabbed the hose-reel from Bob Annis's hands and agitatedly started to wash the petrol away from the van. 'I'll kill the cunt,' he mumbled, closing the spray jet down and blasting the road surface with a direct jet of high-pressure water which in turn sprayed all and sundry.

'He's losing it,' whispered Bob as he passed by to help the sub-officer with the task of washing the road down. Jeff and Vic finally burnt through the twisted steel and iron and slowly eased the screaming driver from the wreckage. His foot was hanging by a thin strand of flesh and sinew to his leg and although the boys had used every bit of their experience, the back of the gaping wound had been seared by the intense heat of the cutting gear. 'Sorry, Guv, best we could do,' said Jeff as they helped the ambulance crew to lay him on the stretcher.

'I want to see you when we get back, Sub,' said Silvers as he climbed into the cab, 'in my office.' The pump and the ET pulled away, leaving the PE's crew to finish up and give details to the police.

As we drove back in the usual uneasy silence after this sort of job, I tried to lighten things a little. 'No need to have got that worked up, Bert, my bike wasn't worth that much anyway.' The sub-officer's total disregard for my comment only brought home to me the utter futility of any remarks when we attended incidents so tragic in their outcome. By now I started to shiver as the consciousness of my wringing wet gear against my skin began to take over from the protection it had been afforded by the surge of adrenaline at the incident.

We had another half-hour of the shift remaining and the majority of the watch had assembled in the rec room. Jeff was behind the bar of the Long Branch, checking the stock and till with Laurie Shelly of the Red watch before handing over to him.

'How'd the medical go, Lul?' Fireman Shelly was a tall man, well over six feet, with dark black hair combed back with plenty of Brylcream, Denis Compton style. He had a large protruding nose and huge hands which added to his somewhat comical appearance.

'Bad news, Jeff,' he replied in his usual laconic way, which hid a rich vein of sharp humour. 'The Doc told me the back's in a pretty bad way, really upset me 'e did. Said I'd never be able to do skydiving, skiing, mountain climbing, or muff diving. Still, three out of four ain't bad, is it?' Laurie was in his mid-forties; his slow drawl and even slower pace of walking endeared him to everyone. 'We've got a new recruit on our watch. Did you 'ear about the other night?' Jeff shook his head in anticipation of the latest initiation tale. 'Told the silly little sod he was on fire watch duty. We sent 'im up to the top of the tower wiv a flask, blanket and a pair of binoculars, looking for fires, can you believe it? He stayed up there all bloody night. Like a frozen turd when 'e came down this morning.' Laurie's cheeks seemed to get even redder as he burst into laughter at the junior buck's ordeal.

At least this recruit had managed to hang on to his dignity – others had been lowered stark naked into the deep well pit in the station yard and submerged into ice-cold water. One even earned the nickname 'Winkle', because of his shrivelled appendage. Everyone in the job seemed to collect a nickname, some stupid, but others quite clever. I was once introduced to a member of another watch and told his name was 'Dickado'. It turned out that when asked his name, he replied, 'Richard, but Dick'll do.'

A few weeks later I was to experience my first twenty-pump fire. A four-storey warehouse on London's ground in Bow had caught light and they had requested help from West Ham. Two pumps were sent to the scene, one from Plaistow and another from Silvertown. We handed our nominal roll boards into the control unit, a Bristol single-decker converted coach with a crash gearbox, with which I was to become only too familiar later.

The officer in charge ordered our crews on to what was left of the top floor. After climbing the external steel staircase, we entered the shell of the building. All three floors had totally collapsed on to the ground floor, leaving only steel joists, which were to be our means of crossing from one wall to another. Two turntable ladders were pumping gallons of water from their vantage point above what used to be the roof. Our task was to man four two-and-a-half inch hose lines to cool and extinguish any seats of fire that may erupt. We managed to find a corner of the floor that hadn't burnt away and proceeded to carry out our task.

'Typical bloody London job, they've got enough bodies 'ere to stamp the bleedin' fire out.'

'You're not impressed then, Paddy,' said Daisy.

Station Officer McGinty shook his head. 'Can you imagine it when this lot take over in April? Bloody disaster.' The combination of steam and choking acrid smoke welling up from the debris below began to affect our breathing.

'Sod this, let's move over to the other side,' said Vic, coughing violently. He walked precariously over the steel girder with a hundred foot line slung on his shoulder. 'You next, Hooligan,' I peered down into the black, suffocating abyss. Luckily I couldn't see a bloody thing, which was a blessing really, as my bravado would probably have been severely dampened had I seen the drop below. I made my way cautiously to the other side and threw the line back in order to pull the hose across. Vic and I pressed our backs against the wall and began spraying water on to one of the remaining walls in order to cool it down, hopefully preventing a possible collapse. Water seemed to be cascading off every joist and wall as I peered down through the smoke. As water from the TLs' jets ploughed into the burning debris below, small pockets of clear air materialised every now and then allowing partial vision of those working below.

'That's Silvers down there, talking to one of their DOs.'

Vic peered down into the mist. 'Yeah, you're right. What's that little sod up to?'

'Getting bloody wet by the looks of things,' I said wryly.

'Well, a little more won't 'urt, then, will it?' I looked on in total amazement as Vic pushed the front flaps of his tunic aside, undid his fly buttons, removed his dick proudly from his pants and proceeded to piss over Silvers who was obviously totally unaware due to the spraying he was already receiving from the jets. Vic must have drunk plenty of tea that day as it seemed to go on for ever, much to the delight of Paddy McGinty and his crew on the other side. Vic's aim was spot on. The direct hit splashed on to the station officer's white combed black helmet and cascaded on to the shoulders of his tunic. He was totally oblivious to his predicament, wrongly assuming that the soaking he was getting was exclusively from the spray of the jets. 'I can now proudly say that I pissed on that little bleeder from a great height.' Vic shook his penis slowly and joyously, before replacing it in his trousers.

The nice thing about being on a large job with London was that you could be certain their brigade tea van would be somewhere on site. We were relieved of our duties by a crew from Burdett Road station and made a dash for the van before Silvers could prevent us from our refreshment. The tea and biscuits always seemed far superior to anything back at the station.

'Ah, there you are! I might have guessed.' Silvers placed his elbow on the counter of the van and ordered tea and biscuits for himself.

'You look a bit wet, Guv, you'll catch pneu-bleedin'-monia if you're not careful,' said Vic as if deeply concerned about Silvers's welfare. The station officer wiped his hand on the shoulder of his tunic before picking up his biscuit, much to our amusement, and looked at Vic quizzically.

'You taking the piss, old Evans?' Fragments of biscuit splattered from the side of his mouth on to Daisy's tunic. Dave wiped them off frantically.

'No, Guv, just concerned about your welfare,' replied Vic. Silvers was perplexed at our obvious amusement.

'Something funny, old O'Halloran?' He slammed his cup down on the counter. 'Come on, let's go.' He stormed off back to the engines amid gales of laughter from the other crews, who had by now been informed on the 'jungle drums' of Fireman Evans's endeavour.

★

Station Officer Silvers somehow managed to find out about Vic's indiscretion, but without witnesses could do little about it. He spent the next few shifts trying to pin something on Vic, but to no avail, and so he reverted to form and singled Fireman Evans out for every shitty job that came up, whether it was on the fire ground or at the station. On one occasion he even took to physically assaulting Vic. We had an old large brown enamel teapot, that was heated up on the gas ring then placed on the table for all to help themselves. Silvers was always last into the mess room, and would push his way past the occupied chairs to reach the teapot. He dragged the hot pot across the Formica top and deliberately grazed it along Vic's uncovered forearm.

'Jesus bleedin' Christ! Vic shot up out of his chair, rubbing his arm furiously.

'Oh, was that your arm, old Evans, sorry.' The snide grin on the station officer's face conveyed only too well that his action was intended. Silvers continued to pour his tea and then sat down at the head of the table with an air of self-satisfaction. Vic had gone into the kitchen to run his arm under the cold tap.

'You all right, Vic?' queried the cook.

'I'll get that little bastard.' She passed him a towel and he wrapped it around the arm. 'I'll 'ave 'im , don't you worry.'

It was some weeks after the event when most of us had forgotten the incident, that Fireman Evans invoked his revenge. The teapot was, as usual, in the middle of the table and the station officer was once again the last to arrive. 'Is he still in the office, Smiffy?' The watch room man nodded his head. 'Good.' Vic snatched the teapot off the table and rushed it into the kitchen. 'Give me a nod when he's coming, Woodsie.' Daisy poked his head through the open mess room window. Vic slid the saucepan, that the cook was preparing for lunch, off the front gas ring and placed the black handle of the enamel pot directly over the flame. Several minutes passed before Dave gave the alarm that Silvers was coming. Vic wrapped an oven cloth around the spout and rushed the pot back into the centre of the table, collapsing into his chair as Silvers entered the door. The anticipating silence in the mess room should have given the station officer an inkling that something was amiss, but he proceeded to march towards the teapot. Alan shuffled his chair to one side in preparation of any misdirected spillage.

'You're all right, old Cobby, don't move.' Alan disregarded the advice and continued to ease his chair to one side. Bob Annis's face started to grimace as Silvers's outstretched hand reached for the pot. I had my teeth clenched tight as his hand encompassed the searing hot handle. The intake of air as the cook gasped from behind the serving hatch was clearly audible in the eerie silence. There was only a slight twitch from the corner of Silvers's mouth as he continued to raise the teapot, before pouring it into his mug. The pot was then hurriedly placed back on to the table as he snatched the mug into his other hand and rushed out into the yard towards his office, his jaw clenched tight.

'Can you smell burning flesh?' inquired Jeff. Nobody answered, but there was a distinct odour present that wasn't there a few minutes before.

'Got 'im!' shouted Vic triumphantly, thrusting his fist into the air.

'Christ, he didn't even flinch,' said Dave in astonishment.

'He knew he'd been had – the little sod didn't want you lot to gloat,' said Jeff. 'Could be all-out war now, Vic.'

Chapter Thirteen

The sub-officer closed the rec room door as he entered the room and sat down on one of the foot lockers. 'All packed?' he continued, patting the large khaki canvas kit bag in front of my locker. I nodded my assurance. 'Good, well now you can bloody well unpack it, because the old man wants me to do an inventory and check that all your gear is marked with your name and number.'

'What about Daisy and Alan?' I retorted.

'Already checked theirs,' Bert replied, undoing the drawstring at the top of my bag.

'Bastard!'

'Who, me?' Bert said, pointing to himself.

'No, that nasty little bugger in there,' I said, pulling the contents from the bag. Bert smiled as I pulled the last item from the kit bag and threw the shoes on to my bed. 'Just a minute – when did you check their gear?'

Alan and Daisy started to make a hasty retreat as the realisation that I had been well and truly tucked up dawned on me. 'Right, that's it.' I rushed out into the ablutions and filled a galvanised bucket up with water. By this time the whole watch had hastily retreated into the station yard, expecting, as I thought, to avoid getting wet. I rushed blindly out into the yard to be met by the sight of four lines of hose, connected to the pump and pump escape and aimed directly at me.

'Oh, shit!'

I turned to run back into the toilets as the drivers started the pumps up. I shook the door handle feverishly and then began kicking the bottom of the door as the realisation that the grinning bastard at the window, my so-called friend, Jeff Burnett, had bolted the door. 'I'll get you, Burnett.' My cries were drowned as the full force of the jets pinned me to the wall. I tried vainly to get my breath, as four hundred gallons of water per minute started to slowly wash me towards the ground.

By now I was thoroughly soaked and the one hundred and fifty pounds per square inch pressure from each of the four jets was beginning to take its toll on my aching body. In situations of adversity one has to protect what is dear to one and therefore covering my testicles seemed the appropriate action to take. The pump operators eased the pressure down slowly as they disengaged the pumps.

'You all right, Hooligan?' Bert eased me gently to my feet. 'We knew you'd go for the water, we were banking on that.'

Fireman Burnett was still up at the toilet window, grinning like a Cheshire cat. Revenge was going to be very sweet! We said our goodbyes at change of watch and made our way across the yard towards our cars.

'Burnetts in the bog having a crap, Jim, just thought you'd like to know.'

Vic winked at me and pointed to the pump still in the yard. Daisy ran the hose out for me and Vic volunteered to be the pump operator.

Jeff emerged from the toilet and proceeded to wash his hands at the sink. He turned the taps off and casually looked into the mirror above the sink. The sheer terror in his eyes far surpassed anything we may have been through on that ship, as he perceived the image of me with a fully charged hose in my hand. He frantically started to turn the taps on again; God knows what he thought he was going to achieve as the full force of the jet struck him on his shoulder, spinning him around and trapping him in the corner of the room. The fading cries of 'you rotten Irish bastard' as he sank to the floor were going to be a treasured memory of my spell at Plaistow.

Chapter Fourteen

It was the first of April 1965, the formation of the new GLC. As I drove past the Princess Alice at Forest Gate it brought back memories of my childhood. Kenny Cox, myself and Dennis Chipperfield would emerge from the Saturday morning picture show at the Odeon opposite and clamber over the wall and down into the bomb site of the old Alice. There we would re-enact the saga of Hopalong Cassidy. I would be Hoppy of course, simply because I could beat the other two up. Kenny would be Lucky and Dennis would be Gabby Hayes. We would play there for hours, slapping our backsides, riding our imaginary horses, shooting each other and then miraculously releasing one another from death by a mere touch of the hand.

'You're released.'

'No you're not, you're dead.' It usually concluded by 'Lucky' failing arse over tip and cutting his head open once again.

'K-k-Kenny's c-c-cut 'is 'ead open a-a-again, Mrs Cox.'

'I can see what he's done, thank you, Dennis.' Kenny must have had his own cuts man at Queen Mary's Hospital, he'd been there so many times.

I drove past the Pigeons pub and turned right into Stratford's yard. Alan's Rover 100 was already parked. Like everything Alan possessed, it was immaculate. He would meticulously service and clean it during stand-down periods, unlike my wreck. I staggered across the yard with my kit bag and went directly to the station office to get a locker allocated. Everywhere was clean, bright and shining, unlike Plaistow.

'After roll call, I'll do an inventory check with you, O'Halloran.' Docherty's accent was not the usual harsh Scottish accent portrayed in films and on the telly; it was almost comforting.

'Are you winding me up?'

He peered at me disbelievingly. 'No, I am not winding you up, O'Halloran, I don't wind people up.' I thought back to my first spell with Sub-Officer Docherty and remembered that this quiet-spoken, religious man expected to be treated as he would treat others and that therefore my suggestion was misplaced. I looked into his steely grey eyes and wondered if he had a sense of humour. Six sharp short rings of the call bells brought me back from the pondering of my new mentor. He picked his soft cap off the desk and covered his bald head. He tugged at the corners of his reefer jacket to bring the edges into some form of symmetry with his immaculately pressed trousers.

'Come on, O'Halloran, let's get you reintroduced to the rest of the watch. You know most of them, but there's a couple of new faces been transferred from other watches.'

Roll call was taken by Docherty in the presence of Station Officer Rumford, who was due to be promoted to assistant divisional officer later that year. Most of the names the sub-officer called out were familiar, save one, Fireman Tisi. We checked the appliances, our BA sets and ancillary gear, did the necessary bookings and made our way to the mess room upstairs.

'It's ages since I've slid down poles,' said Alan as we sat down at the table. Stratford only had the two floors, ground and first, whilst some of the older London stations had five or six.

'Think yourself lucky, old 'un, you'd need a strong pair of brown cords if you were at Lambeth.'

Lambeth Fire Station was the headquarters of the London Fire Brigade and as a trainee I had my initial training in the art of sliding down poles there. Some of the drops were staggered, but covered two floors at a time.

'I've no intention of going the other side of Bow Bridge,' Alan replied ruefully.

I looked across the table at the curly-headed young man, Tisi. His countenance would best be described as cherubic, angelic almost. He was in his early twenties, possibly his late teens, about five foot ten inches and squarely built.

'Have you got a brother, Tony Tisi?' I asked.

'Yes, do you know him?'

'I went to Saint Bonaventure's. We were in the same class,' I replied.

I remembered now; the young man sitting opposite me was Christopher, the younger of the Tisi brothers. I had spent many happy times around the Italian family's house in Manbey Park Road, where their mother, who still spoke Italian, would feed most of the altar boys from St Francis's Church. Jim Docherty smiled wryly.

'You see, O'Halloran, I'm trying to get as many left-footers on to my watch as possible, then we can have our own little band of the Knights of St Columbus.'

'I suppose you'll start going round with the bloody plate, then,' chirped Gordon Bliss.

'We'll have to go round twice, Gordon – that's the only way you can be certain it's a Catholic service,' Chris Tisi replied. Although they were a very devout family, I was reminded from the remark that Chris had just made that the Tisis were not averse to the self-mocking Catholic or Italian joke. At least it would take some of the flak from me.

It amazed me that within the fire service, I had discovered that most of the racist jokes were made by the 'ethnics' about themselves. The leading fireman on this particular watch now was 'Jake' Jacobson, of obvious Jewish extraction, who was to keep us up half the night with a flood of Jewish jokes. 'Heard about the Jewish caterer who vanted an audience vith de Pope to give him the bill for the Last Supper!' Jake was a huge man, over six feet tall, with a mop of black curly hair topping his jolly round face. 'I must be the only Yid in the East End doing manual work – all the rest are taxi drivers or running the rag trade.' His large belly would shake uncontrollably as he derived as much enjoyment from his quotes and jokes as the rest of the watch.

'Does your dad still sharpen knives, Chris?' I asked. Mr Tisi had an old three-wheeled cycle, which had a huge grinding stone in the barrow section, and he used to tour the East End putting a fine hone on people's cutlery. The back wheel would be jacked up and the pedal power used to turn the grinding stone. 'Yes, he still does it,' replied Chris.

'Makes a change from flogging ice cream.' Jake shook visibly at his reference to the numerous Italian ice cream vendors in the area.

'What do you think of the bar, Hooligan?' Gordon pointed to the well-stocked bar which backed on to the partition wall of the kitchen and spread halfway across the rec room floor. I nodded my approval. 'Fancy helping out behind the bar, Jim?' Gordon continued.

'He'll be too busy studying the drill book for his Leading Fireman's practical.' Chris Rumford had entered the dining room, an atlas tucked under his arm ready for a topography lecture. He dropped the book on to the plastic-topped table. 'Won't you, O'Halloran?' The threatening glance from his face forced an affirmative 'Yes, Guv,' from me. Station Officer Rumford hadn't quite forgiven me for my first watch room incident at the old station. I felt my every move was now going to be monitored by the station officer and his second in command, the ginger screw. He drew a large cross on the bottom left hand corner of the blackboard and then proceeded to draw two vertical lines from that point to the top of the board. 'That's Wanstead Flats,' he said, pointing to the cross, 'and that's Capel Road. Name the roads off Capel Road.' He peered around the room, hesitated, as though giving careful thought to the intended choice of victim and then snapped, 'O'Halloran.' He threw the chalk into my lap. Jake grinned as I passed by him, expecting me to make a complete fool of myself.

'Forest Side, Barwick, Chestnut, Cranmer, Latimer, Lorne, Tylney, Ridley.' I continued to rattle off the side streets to the top of the board and finished with a contemptuous flick of the chalk into the air as I made my way back past Jake and into the armchair.

Chris Rumford had a defeated grin on his face as he rubbed the names off the board. 'Someone's put you up to this, O'Halloran?'

'No, sir, I've just been very diligent, not wasted my study periods.' Luckily the call bells saved me from deeper interrogation. Some of the watch scrambled for the safety of the stairs whilst the remainder used the pole house to reach the appliance bay.

'Studying, my arse! 'Ow come you knew those roads, Hooligan?' Gordon pushed my backside into the rear cab of the pump escape as he scrambled in beside me.

'I did most of my courting around that area. Joan lived just across the flats in Forest Road,' I replied with a smirk of self-satisfaction.

'You jammy sod.'

The escape screeched to a halt halfway down West Ham Lane. We had been called to a road traffic accident involving a Routemaster bus. An ambulance was already on the scene as we disembarked. The mangled rear wheel and part of a push-bike chassis were protruding from the near-side front wheel of the bus.

'What have we got, mate?'

The ambulance man looked in anguish at Chris Rumford.

'It's a small kid – he's pinned by his arm and shoulder under the wheel, still conscious, looks nasty, though.'

The station officer didn't have to relate his intentions. The blocks and jacks were already being positioned as he lay flat on his stomach to assess the situation. 'It's all right, son, we'll soon have you out.' I manoeuvred the jack under the front axle. Blocks were placed fore and aft on all the wheels.

'Make sure the handbrake's on,' Docherty shouted to Alan as I started to slowly lever the jack handle up and down. 'Get those blocks under the axle.' The boy was about nine or ten and although fully conscious was unable to speak through sheer shock. Jake and Chris had crawled under the bus from the other side and were encouraging the boy with words of comfort. 'I reckon you'll get a new bike after this,' Jake said, trying to lighten the situation. That's a fucking stupid statement, I thought, as I gingerly pushed down on to the lever, raising the bus another fraction of an inch. I would think that's the last thing his parents would want to buy him after this. Gordon wedged another block under the axle as the bus slowly rose off the boy's arm. It was a real mess. The bus must have braked violently as he fell underneath. The front wheel had locked with the child pinned underneath by his arm and shoulder, and the bus had obviously skidded some distance with the boy still trapped under the wheel as there was a four foot trail of crushed bone and blood embedded into the road surface under the chassis.

'All right, Daisy?' Alan had joined Dave, who was now assisting Gordon with the wooden blocks.

'Yes, I'm fine, Al.'

'Good boy,' Alan patted Fireman Woods on the back and slid back on to the pavement to assist the ambulance men with the stretcher. The boy started to groan as daylight appeared between the bottom of the tyre and the remains of his arm. 'Get some sort of tourniquet at the top of his arm. When we lift this there's going to be a lot of claret about.'

'Okay, son, were nearly there.' Jim Docherty slipped his arm under the boy's back, ready to assist the ambulance men. They had already checked him over and had established that apart from the arm and shoulder he had sustained just a few minor cuts and bruises. 'Just a couple of more inches.'

Now that the pressure was off his arm I was able to use the lever more aggressively. 'Come on you bastard, move!'

The station officer waved his arm, 'Okay, okay, that's it, we can get to him now.' There were a couple of feeble groans from the boy as he was gently lifted and slid towards the waiting stretcher. By now the poor little bugger had given up and he slipped quietly into unconsciousness. The pressure from the weight of the bus on his limb had prevented any great loss of blood and once the ambulance crew had attended to what remained of his arm, he was quickly removed to Queen Mary's Hospital, just a few yards away. We waited for the police to mark out the position of the bus and then lowered it back on to the road. It was then driven forward to enable us to scrub and wash, what used to be a child's arm down the drain. I stared at the mash of powdered bone and flesh and for the first time in my career felt physically sick.

'You all right, Hooligan?' Daisy's interjection jolted me from staring at the stain on the road. I nodded feebly. Christ! that's rich – Daisy asking if I'm all right. Come on, O'Halloran, get a grip on yourself, you big tart.

We stowed the appliances and returned to the station. 'Remind me to give the hospital a bell later, Sub.' Docherty acknowledged Chris Rumford's remark and then continued with the topography lecture.

Over the next few uneventful weeks I managed to get down to studying the drill book and with the assistance of the watch and in particular Jim Docherty, I was able to shout my way through numerous practical drills in the station yard. My promotion prospects would be enhanced if I gained other qualifications, and when Station Officer Rumford called me into the office and offered me the chance to become a brigade driver, I jumped at the opportunity. I was temporarily seconded back to Plaistow, which following the change had become a command training school as well as a fire station. The heavy goods course would mean that I was now on permanent day shifts, five days each week with weekends off, which initially pleased Joan until she discovered that trying to drive anywhere at weekends was a waste of time. We were better off having days off during the week.

Three other trainees and myself were instructed in the mechanics of fire engine construction and maintenance, shown numerous physical examples of engines and gearboxes cut in working halfsections and were advised that the brigade were gradually going over to synchromesh gearboxes. This was something that I would be eternally grateful for as I was about to discover on the course. The art of double-declutching on crash gears (so suitably named) on the ridiculous one in three hills around Crystal Palace was to become an albatross around our necks. The gearstick had to be moved from its original position by dipping the clutch and pushing into neutral. Then the correct amount of revs were to be applied, done by listening to the engine (no such thing as bloody rev counters in these clapped-out training vehicles) then, theoretically, once this was obtained, the gearstick could then move to the next position. By the time you had made several frantic attempts at this manoeuvre, and sheared off numerous pieces of metal from the geared cogs, you were now freewheeling suicidally down a quiet residential 1 in 3 'mountain' with bulging forearms trying to grapple with an offset steering wheel that was light years away from the luxury of power steering. As you gathered momentum, the whooshing sound of the vehicles parked on either side and the demented screaming of the instructor only increased the state of sheer panic that was enveloping you. The brakes must have been designed as an aid for the development of thigh and calf muscles in the Charles Atlas body-building course. Power assisted? My arse! That was still twenty years away.

There were less frantic periods as the course progressed, some nice little rides into the Essex countryside, to frighten the living bejesus out of the local farmers who had the audacity to get stuck in front of a fire engine on an impassable country lane. Wonderful what a few sharp rings on a fire bell can do. Towards the end of my training we had occasion to drive down Forest Road, where most of my courting was done – number 19, front room, lying on the floor, listening to Lonnie Donegan, whilst feverishly trying to undo Joan's bra before her mum entered with the tea and eventually sent me scampering to catch the last train at Forest Gate station.

Percy was cutting the privet edge protruding above the green and white painted wicket fence as the fire engine pulled up outside. He removed his chequered flat cap off his head and wiped his brow with his forearm.

'My Christ, I've seen it all now.'

'Seen what?' enquired the instructor.

''Im driving a bloody fire engine,' Percy replied, pointing towards me. 'I never thought he'd stick the fire brigade, too bleedin' soft! He's surprised me, I tell yer.' I don't know who felt the most proud, me or my father-in-law.

We managed to mangle our way through the gearboxes of a 1949 Dennis F7 and a 1954 Dennis F12 before graduating on to a 1955 AEC/Merryweather and finally on to the workhorse of the London Fire Brigade, the Dennis F101. The commander in charge of the driving schools, a certain 'Knocker' White, duly signed to the effect that we had all passed with flying colours. Coming from a man who allegedly was renowned for his partiality to pink gins and, when giving advice when asked what to do in a skid, would reply 'Don't get into one, laddie,' this should have made my watch back at Stratford, a little apprehensive upon my return.

For the first few shifts, I was allowed to drive the fire engines back to the station from incidents. The unfortunate Sub-Officer Docherty seemed to be singled out by Chris Rumford to sit beside me on these occasions. 'If ye hit anythin', O'Halloran, the penance ye got at St Francis is goin' tae appear very lenient, d'ye understand my meaning?' I managed to steer clear of any disasters before being let loose on the real thing. I say managed to steer clear, with one notable exception. The Eastern Command headquarters had its own allocation of senior officer drivers at Stratford, but when shortages occurred through sickness or holidays we were sometimes seconded to assume the duty of driving the black saloon cars. I was in the process of washing and leathering off one such Ford Zephyr when the bells went down for Stratford's engines. Gordon Bliss swung on the rope pulleys to open the double-fronted bay doors, and as the drivers revved up, waiting for Chris Rumford and Jim Docherty, I decided to lend a hand by going on to the forecourt and into the road to hold up any approaching traffic. I turned my back and stuck my arms out officiously as the pump and pump escape roared on to the forecourt, chrome bells clanging their warning. Chris Tisi's grimacing face should have forewarned me of the chaos about to erupt behind my back. As the engines swung past me, the clattering of metallic bumpers and breaking glass from the four-car pile-up slowly drowned out the fading noise of the bells. I stood there for a few moments, still facing in the opposite direction to the carnage behind and waited for Chris and Tom to race out and inspect the damage. 'No one's hurt, Hooligan, you'd better go in now and hope to Christ nobody tells the ginger screw.'

My first drive in anger was not on the engines but on the old half-cab single-decker Bristol control unit. This ponderous converted bus had flashing blue lights above the destination panel, which now read LONDON FIRE BRIGADE CONTROL UNIT in case we were hailed down at bus stops, and a driver's cab totally isolated from the 'passengers' save for a sliding glass panel behind the driver's head where instructions were bawled at you above the noise of the bell and engine.

'Turn next left, Jim,' screamed the station officer, into the back of my head. 'Where?' I yelled back, crashing more metal filings into the gear box as I attempted to double-declutch for the umpteenth time.

'Next left,' he bawled once more. I had long since lost my bearings; in fact, once we had passed the London Hospital, I was entirely in his hands.

'Do you think we can turn the lights and bell off,' I yelled. 'It's bloody embarrassing – push-bikes are passing us now!'

'Keep going, you're doing great, best drive we've had for ages.'

'Are you taking the piss?' He assured me he wasn't, and once we reached our destination, the rest of the crew congratulated me. I later found out this was due to the fact that none of their maps, pencils, books and papers had fallen from the purpose-built cupboards. It apparently took them ages to restow the beast after a shout.

There had been a tradition in the job to undertake various charitable events in order to raise money for the Fire

Services National Benevolent Fund, and one such occasion at the Windsor public house in Canning Town had been organised on our next rest day.

Joan and I parked around the back of the pub and then made our way round to the front entrance. It was a funny little place from the outside, only about thirty feet across in a terraced block of shops and various small industrial units. Upon entering we found it to be even more peculiar. The width remained the same throughout the ninety foot depth. Most of the boys had already arrived along with their companions and had settled down amongst the mixture of regulars: dockies, local residents and a group of old ladies at the far end huddled round a huge oblong table.

'Plonk yourself down here, Joan.' Vic Evans offered his seat up to Joan.

'That's all right, Vic.'

'Do as yer bleedin' well told.' She smiled and took up the vacant chair. The fund's collecting tins were lined up on the table, ready to be rattled under the noses of the customers once we had entertained them. I say we, but I had it on good authority that Tom Delarue was to be the star attraction of the evening. A space was being cleared in the middle of the floor in expectation of the cabaret show.

'I didn't know Tom done this sort of thing, what's he do exactly?'

'Don't even ask, Hooligan, we'll be lucky to get out of this place alive later,' replied Gordon. A few of the lights were turned down and a spot beamed at the space on the floor.

'Ladies and gentle bleedin' men, please put your hands together for the great Chief Hiawatha.'

I looked quizzically at Daisy, who shrugged his shoulders in disbelief.

'Oh shit,' groaned Bert, 'Better get the bloody first-aid box out, this could be nasty.' The six foot plus frame, shrouded entirely in a grey fire brigade blanket save for a plume of exposed feathers, glided on to the floor. The record 'Running Bear' blared out from the Dansette record player as Tom started to hop around the floor in his own variation of the Indian war dance. The blanket was dramatically discarded. A mixture of shock and amazement caused the old ladies to gasp loudly as they were exposed to the sight of this extremely white Red Indian prancing around with his genitals covered by a hastily conceived loincloth.

'I knew I was two chamois leathers light at the station.' McGinty thumped the table in annoyance. 'I've been looking everywhere for them.'

My mouth was still hanging wide open in total disbelief when Vic announced that we were to be treated to the greatest display of fire-eating and pain endurance we were ever likely to witness. Four lads from Silvertown grabbed some water extinguishers and placed them ominously at strategic points around the floor. 'Jesus, I hope they haven't taken them off the station as well,' moaned McGinty, grabbing one of the extinguishers to check the station identity number. A sigh of relief exuded from Paddy's broad frame as he replaced the extinguisher. Tom had now grabbed two large poles which were smothered in methylated spirit and he began to wave them gingerly over his arms and torso.

'I can't smell any hairs burning this time,' Jeff said disappointedly.

Tom was now swigging out of the bottle Vic had passed to him, and with a theatrical flourish brought the burning pole across his face as he spat the methylated spirit from his mouth. 'Ooh... aah.' The old ladies were certainly impressed as the vaporised flame flashed across the room towards them.

'Where did he learn all this from?' I asked.

'From his spell with Monty in Africa. He hasn't collared you yet, but you'll hear all about his war exploits,' replied Gordon. 'Walter Mitty's got sod all on Tom.' Docherty smiled, almost sympathetically, towards me.

'And now for your enter bleedin' tainment, the dreaded bed of nails.'

The old ladies clapped enthusiastically as the apparatus was dragged on to the floor. 'Can we have one volunteer, please.' One of the old ladies tried to make it on to the floor, but was beaten by the biggest oriental seaman I've ever seen. From the look on Tom's face, this guy was definitely not first choice. Tom laid his frame on to the sheet of hardboard, the six inch nails protruding ominously into his back. He wiped his hand across his forehead wiping a profusion of sweat on to the floor. 'Sit on 'im Chang,' yelled one of the seaman's mates. The massive sailor was persuaded by Vic that this was not the way forward with the entertainment. He was gently assisted to stand on Tom's chest. Fireman Delarue expanded his chest and held his breath as the sailor let go of Vic's helping hand. 'A big round of applause, ladies and gentlemen, please.' Vic turned towards the audience to invite the appreciation, and while his back was turned the sailor jumped up and down on Tom's chest. Tom's breath was violently forced front his chest as he sat bolt upright, causing the assailant to stumble to the floor.

'Oi, you chinky bastard, I'll do you,' screamed McGinty. Vic spun round in time to stop Paddy from grabbing the seaman. The table of seamen rose from their chairs in unison with the firemen in the room.

As the protagonists rushed towards each other, a loud crashing sound echoed around the pub as the landlord smashed a builder's shovel against a steel column by the bar. 'Right!' he bawled. 'If you're not back in your seats by the time I count to ten, me and my assistants will be forced to assist you back.' Half a dozen throwbacks to prehistoric times swarmed around their guv'nor.

'Come on lads, let's have some common sense, Tom's all right.' McGinty pointed towards Delarue. 'No harm's been done. Tom's going to continue.' Gordon was wiping the small pinpricks of blood off Tom's back with a towel.

'Chief Hiawatha will now perform with the death-defying glass pillow,' Vic continued, trying to take some of the steam out of the situation.

He now picked up an empty bottle from our table, walked casually over to the seamen and duly smashed it down on to their table, shattering it into fragments. He quickly smiled at them, held his arms up in a gesture of surrender and wiped the glass pieces off the table and into a large sack. 'Any more?' With that request, numerous bottles were discarded into the sack, which Vic tied at the top then stamped on, crushing the glass inside. 'Can we have quiet, please.' The pub was agog as the 'pillow' was placed under Tom's head. Tom rolled the back of his head gingerly over the sack and then sat bolt upright. He took a deep breath and then threw himself backwards, crashing his head down on the pillow. The sickening thud redoubled around the room. 'Jesus Christ!' Joan gripped my hand and Kay covered her mouth with her hand. Before the audience could adjust, Tom had jumped up into a kneeling position and commenced to head-butt the pillow furiously with his forehead. He jumped to his feet as the strains of 'Running Bear' began once more, and milked every bit of applause and adoration from the old ladies and sailors alike.

'Quick, get round with the tins now,' shouted Bert Cross, as Tom disappeared to change. Everyone seemed to have enjoyed the cabaret, judging by the amount of money being pushed into the tins.

'Is there any more?' enquired one old lady.

'No, that's it love,' replied Bert, 'but we'll probably have a bloody good sing-song once we've downed enough of these,' pointing towards the pints of bitter lined up on the table.

'Oh, luv'ly, I like the old songs best,' she said, hastily pouring the remains of her Cream Label stout into her mouth, thereby more or less obliging Bert to buy her another. He dug his hand grudgingly into his pocket and walked towards the bar.

'I see Bert's pulled,' quipped Vic.

'If he hasn't, he will in a minute – Dock Yard Doris has just walked in with Mucky Molly.' The two ladies referred to by Paddy McGinty were notorious for their 'special' care and concern for wayward merchant seamen around the docks, and could be seen regularly at the dock gates greeting the new arrivals or guiding them towards the Graving Dock Tavern and other local hostelries in order to ply their trade. Doris was in her early thirties, English, with a mop of curled blond hair in the Marilyn Monroe style. She was slightly built, whilst her dark-haired Irish companion was a lady of more mature years and better endowed in the bust and bum department.

'Bert, ye old fecker, how are ye?'

Bert looked somewhat bemused. 'I'm sorry, madam, I don't believe I have the honour.'

'Aw come on, ye little scallywag, don't be shy in front of your friends.' She made a quick grab for Bert's wedding tackle, which he tried to avoid but without success. He hurriedly placed his pint back on the counter and turned his attention to the vice-like grip being applied to his balls.

'Christ Almighty, let go, will yer.'

'Someone's always grabbing your nuts, Bert, what is it wiv you?' smiled Jeff.

'You've put 'er up to this, Burnett, you bastard, get 'er off me!' Molly smiled and released her grip on Bert's genitals. 'Christ, I pity those poor bleedin' sailors if they don't come across with 'er.' Bert walked over to our table, gently caressing his crutch. Molly and Doris went about their trade, trying to pick on some poor seaman who'd had a skinful and wouldn't realise he'd been fleeced until he awoke the next morning with a severe hangover. Tom emerged from a door behind the bar, acknowledging the cheers from his new-found admirers, and made his way over to us.

'Do you mind Bert! In front of the ladies!' Tom pointed to our wives and girlfriends, who in fact were ignoring Bert's belated attempts to ease the pain of his scrotum by rubbing his hand up and down inside his trousers.

'Sit down here, Tom,' I said admiringly.

'Christ, are you all right, Tom?' Kay said, somewhat concerned. Tom was sweating profusely after his monumental efforts, and the small droplets of perspiration on his furrowed brow were now beginning to collect rivulets of blood from the plenitude of minute cuts on his forehead. 'Here, let me wipe your forehead,' said Kay, applying Gordon's hanky to Tom's face.

'Thanks very bleedin' much,' said Gordon, who had given Kay his handkerchief in the belief she required it for herself. As Tom turned towards Kay, it was now obvious that the wounds to his forehead were minor, compared to the 'river' running down from somewhere in his thick Brylcreemed black hair towards his collar.

'Jesus, Tom, we'll have to put a plaster on that bugger,' said Vic, pointing Delarue towards the toilet.

The remainder of the evening went reasonably well, a great amount of money was raised for charity and the old ladies in the snug end were being further entertained by Bert, who was by now three sheets to the wind and in full flow.

'They seem to be enjoying themselves,' said Joan.

'Yeah, Bert's found a captive audience,' replied Vic.

As we had our backs to the snug, it was difficult to see what was going on, but every now and then could hear Bert's shrill voice above the crescendos of matronly laughter as tables were being thumped by wrinkled hands with nails brightly varnished red, probably supplied by one of the dubious merchant seamen.

'And now I shall do my Ronnie Ronnald impersonation, followed by some farmyard animals.' The shrill whistling tones of 'If I Were a Blackbird' wafted from the snug as Bert covered the two fingers he had stuffed into his mouth with his other hand. The old ladies broke into spontaneous song as Bert got to the chorus.

'Aw Jasus, he's lovely hands and mouth now,' said Molly as she propped herself up against some poor unsuspecting oriental.

'You speakin' from personal experience, Mol?' quipped Vic. Two fingers were raised towards Vic Evans.

'Feck off.'

'And now for my *pièce de résistance* ladies, my impression of an African elephant!' Bert had hardly time to finish the sentence as about five chairs from around our table were sent crashing to the floor.

'Oh Jesus Christ, no, somebody stop 'im, for Christ's sake,' yelled Jeff, leaping over a fallen chair as he stumbled towards the snug. As most of the watch had reacted instinctively, I felt it my duty to follow the rush towards our sub-officer. The dropped jaws and wide startled eyes of the old ladies, together with the rear view of Bert's trousers with his side pocket linings turned inside out, alerted us to the fact that we were too late.

'Put it away and do your bleedin' flies up,' demanded Alan Cobb as we grabbed Bert and frogmarched him out of the snug.

'We want Bert! We want Bert!' chanted the old girls as we ushered him past the bar towards the bogs. As Bert was held in a vice-like grip by both arms, it had been impossible for him to comply with Alan's demand's. Dockyard Doris jumped out in front of us, dropped to her knees and commenced mouth to penis resuscitation. By now the bar was in uproar, Bert's stupid grin remaining on his face as we dragged Doris off and pushed Bert into the toilets.

'I just hope to God no one reports this to the *Stratford Express*,' Daisy said worriedly. We sobered Bert up as best we could and ordered a cab.

'I'll take him home,' said Tom as he fell into the cab with Bert.

'Christ! You look as though you've 'ad a bloody good night, boys.' The cab driver surveyed the bloodstained countenance of Tom and the contented yet supercilious look of the sub-officer.

Chapter Fifteen

Alan Cobb pushed the mop lazily around the toilet floor whilst recounting the story of 'Godfrey the Ghost' who roamed the old station at Stratford Broadway.

'Did you ever see him, Al?' I asked.

'Nope, but quite a few have.'

I had been telling of my own encounter with Godfrey. It was back at the old station and I was making my way across the station yard to the pump crew dormitory to wake Bill Mumford up for the next two hour watch duty. As I approached the door under the drill tower I noticed a light on in one of the upstairs offices above the dorm. I pushed the door open and made my way towards the dormitory door but was distracted from entering by a phone ringing from upstairs. I then heard a man's voice answering the call. I bypassed the dorm door and proceeded apprehensively up the stone stairs towards the office. The voice continued from inside the room but stopped abruptly when I knocked on the door.

'Hello – is any one there?' There was a slight pause and the voice continued its conversation. I knocked tentatively again. The voice rambled on. What's the worst scenario, O'Halloran, I thought to myself. You burst in and it's the chief officer – another mild bollocking! Go on, go for it! I turned the brass handle slowly, the door creaked open, of course, and I burst into the room. The telephone was off the hook and lying on the desk, and the male voice was no longer. This was really strange, as the only way the phone could have rung was by me, the watch room man, transferring the call. I picked the phone up: dead as a doornail. I placed it gingerly back on to the rest, switched the light off and made my way down to the dormitory.

'Sounds like Godfrey's at it again,' suggested Fireman Mumford as we exchanged our duties. I went across the yard to the boiler room to make sure the boiler was still dampened down and alight. I gave it a good rake and piled about six good shovels of coke into the glowing furnace, told Bill the 'Appy' was okay and made my way back across the yard towards the dormitory. The bloody lights were on again! I dashed upstairs, convinced I was being wound up by some of the insomniacs on the watch. The voice stopped abruptly as I burst into the office. The phone was off the hook again. I searched frantically around the room, under tables, in cupboards, and drawers. Nothing!

'What the fuck's going on up there?' shouted the leading fireman who had obviously been awakened with the rest of the crew by my endeavours. I related my ghostly tale, which was taken with a pinch of salt by some of the crew but taken to heart by others who had also encountered 'Godfrey' and his antics.

'He obviously didn't follow us here,' said Alan, 'but apparently, some of the council staff at the town hall reckon they've seen strange goings on at the old station. Sod it!' Alan plunged the mop into the galvanised bucket as the loud reverberations of the call bell above our heads warned us of our next shout. 'East Ham's ground, Prefabs, Savage Gardens, they're out, four-pumper down the docks.' We grabbed the slips of paper from his hand.

After several 'drives' back from shouts I had now been deemed competent by Chris Rumford to drive to an incident. Sub-Officer Docherty climbed up, tentatively besides me.

'Do you know where you're going, O'Halloran?'

'Yes, Sub.'

'If they're the ones I'm thinking of, Sub, those prefabs are derelict,' shouted Tom Delarue from the back of the cab. Docherty seemed to be ringing the bells with more passion than usual as we progressed along Romford Road towards the 'Alice'. I hadn't realised it was in all probability sheer terror at being sat next to yet another young driver starting out on his driving career.

As we approached the crossroads with Upton Lane and Woodgrange Road, most of the traffic pulled towards one side. I was feeling quiet pleased with myself as the double-declutching and gear changes, at speed, were going like a dream.

'Christ, what's she up to?' shouted Docherty as the green Morris Traveller in front veered from side to side but managed to stay doggedly in our path. He rang the bells frantically, leaned across to the dash and flashed the headlights repeatedly into the rear view mirror of the car. The woman driving accelerated in response but remained in our path.

'I'll go on the other side of the road,' I shouted as we neared the traffic lights.

'You'll stay where you fucking well are!' retorted the sub-officer. 'Christ Almighty!'

Docherty grabbed the dash in front of him to brace himself as the woman in front decided to stop dead. I stood up out of my seat as I brought all the pressure I could bear on to the foot-brake, clutch and frantically the handbrake. First-aid boxes, railway horns, gloves and hearth kit boxes came hurtling past Chris and Tom in the back, through the dividing partition and spewed out on to the engine cowling, bouncing on to the sub-officers boot before finally coming to rest on the floor. We had stopped some two inches away from the chrome bumper of the Morris.

'Everyone okay?' A subdued grunt came from the rear. 'They're still alive,' acknowledged the sub. 'Now you can drive round her, O'Halloran.' I crashed the gears on the Merryweather into first and proceeded to Savage Gardens. 'If you've got your Rosary with you, Tisi, use it,' the sub-officer said wryly to Chris, who was busily replacing the gear being handed to him by Docherty.

The corrugated asbestos roof of the prefabricated house was cracking loudly as the heat and flames exploded towards the sky, scattering large chunks of jagged asbestos around the building. Acrid smoke and flames surged through the broken windows, twisting their heated tongues towards the overgrown bushes devouring the outside walls. 'Find the nearest hydrant – we're going to need plenty of water here. No heroics; we'll fight this from outside.'

The pump beat us to the job and had already started to cascade water on to the roof by way of two hose-reels. Chris and I started to rig a standpipe to the hydrant to augment the supply to the pump.

'Excuse me, mate.' One of the watching neighbours tapped me on the shoulder. 'There's an old tramp who dosses down in there sometimes.'

Docherty immediately ordered Chris and me into the prefab, giving Alan and Daisy time to put on their proto BA sets. Tom and the LF were directed round the back towards the kitchen area. Before entering I had grabbed the two-and-a-half inch hose line that had just been connected to the pump. I pulled back the handle on the brass hand-controlled branch until I achieved a spray of some considerable force.

'Stick close to me, Chris, and watch your head for falling debris.' The force of the water smashed the unlocked front door back on its hinges as billows of acrid black smoke rushed over our heads, engulfing the pump and its opera-tor. Crouching, we made our way forwards, coughing and spluttering as the dense smoke and heat entered our lungs. I aimed the jet towards the ceiling to dislodge any loose debris.

'Shit!' cried Chris as a huge piece of asbestos roof came crashing down in front of us, causing an eruption on the debris already lying on the floor. The water from the jet cleared the atmosphere directly in front of me but Chris was bearing the brunt of the dust and smoke behind.

'You all right, Chris?'

'Yeah, yeah, keep going, Jim.'

'Sodding door's locked,' I spluttered as we came across the door to what I presumed would have been the living room. 'Hold the branch, Chris.' I placed one hand on the frame of the door to steady myself, leaned back, raised my right boot and gave one almighty kick against the door lock. The door flew open and my momentum sent me crashing through the open frame and on to the burning settee. My black helmet had been knocked off at the moment of impact and the embers from the settee had, unknowingly to me, set my hair alight. I raised myself slowly up off the floor only to be knocked arse over tip again as Chris aimed the jet directly at my head. 'For fuck's sake, Tisi, watch what you're doing.'

'Okay, you two, come out now, they've found him,' shouted Chris Rumford. We emerged, eyes and noses running, coughing and inhaling large chunks of fresh air to ease the soreness on our chests. Tom and Daisy, who were in the same 'healthy' state as us, were half-carrying and half-dragging the dishevelled tramp away from the prefab.

'Put him down there,' Chris Rumford pointed to the pavement.

'He's dead,' murmured one of the onlooking neighbours, from across the road.

'He's still breathing! Call for an ambulance,' shouted Docherty.

'Already done,' replied the ever-efficient Fireman Cobb.

The man looked quite elderly, but because of his long matted hair and beard, he was probably much younger than my estimation of late seventies. He had no shoes; his black socks were full of holes and probably not black at all. His tattered trousers and underpants were twisted halfway down his legs, exposing his blackened thighs and genitals. Tom tried in vain to tug them up to prevent further exposure to the onlooking crowd.

'Get a blanket off the machine,' ordered the LF. I placed the blanket gently over the man's lower body.

'Christ, his arms and chest are well burnt,' said Tom as I tried to wipe the 'debris' from his blackened hands. A piece fell away, exposing a finger bone and reddened flesh. 'They're well charred, Jim, just cover them.'

Daisy knelt down beside me; he had obviously learnt to cope with his fainting bouts by now. I fumbled through the matted grey beard and pulled the old man's mouth open. The search for false dentures was unnecessary as the vast majority of teeth were missing and those that remained were a mixture of black and green.

'What are you doing, Hooligan?' said Fireman Delarue disgustedly.

'He's stopped breathing. Quick; I'll hold his nose, you give him mouth to mouth, Tom.'

Tom turned disbelievingly towards me. 'Piss off! You give it to him!' I must admit the idea didn't appeal to me either.

'Here, let's get at him.' Fireman Tisi knelt over the man's head, grabbed his arms and began stretching rhythmically backwards and forwards, causing the man's chest to rise and fall. Tom started to press the man's chest, between Chris's efforts. 'He's started again!' cried Daisy triumphantly. 'Quick, get a set off the PE,' Docherty shouted at me. I slung the BA set over my arm and dashed back to the old man.

'I'll hold his nose this time, Hooligan, you put the mouthpiece in his gob,' Tom said sarcastically. I opened the main valve and forced the rubber mouthpiece into his mouth. The mica valves in the tubes lifted and dropped in time to the old man's breathing; he was at last getting pure oxygen into his lungs.

The ambulance arrived and delivered the casualty to East Ham Memorial hospital. 'Great job,' boasted Tom proudly. 'Pity about your BA set though, Hooligan, don't fancy washing that out when we get back.' I smiled broadly at Toms craggy good looks. 'Wasn't my set Tom, it was yours.' The angered cries of 'Bastard' faded as I walked back to the PE to be greeted by a policeman on a 'Noddy' bike.

'You the driver?' he enquired, taking off his black gauntlet gloves. I nodded. 'You lost a ladder at the "Alice"!'

I turned frantically towards the PE. I could have lost a six foot ladder, a first floor ladder, or a hook ladder but my luck wasn't that good. I had lost the fifty foot wheeled escape ladder. The police officer said that witnesses had seen the ladder gently slide off the back of the PE, roll backwards down Romford Road and came to a halt besides a lamppost.

'How many cars did it hit?' Jim Docherty butted in.

'None; no one hurt, no damage,' replied the police officer. 'We won't be taking further action.'

'Well I bloody well will,' retorted the sub-officer.

Back at the station I was interrogated as to whether I had checked the mechanism which locked the head of the escape ladder at change of watch. Thank God Fireman Cobb had assisted me and could verify that all checks to the engine and equipment were carried out as per the brigade orders. It was later discovered at brigade workshops that metal fatigue had caused the clamp to snap when I braked behind the Morris Traveller. The charge of failing to obey brigade orders was therefore dropped.

★

I finally got rid of the clapped-out Ford Anglia van and replaced it with a 'sit up and beg' blue Ford Poplar, which was to prove to be even more knackered than the Anglia. I parked our new acquisition behind our neighbours' immaculate Hillman Minx, as Corinne came running out to greet me.

'Guess what Daddy? Mummy's had your fire engines here today.'

'My fire engines?'

'Yes, she caught the chimney alight. There were flames coming out of the roof.'

'You mean the chimney, tell-tale,' said Joan as I picked my excited daughter up into my arms and kissed her.

'What happened?' I asked as Joan kissed me on the cheek.

'Don't panic, they weren't from West Ham. It was East Ham's pump; they said they'd keep it quiet to save you any embarrassment.'

I looked at my wife disbelievingly. 'You must be joking. It'll be all round the Command by now.'

Joan put a reassuring arm round my waist as we walked down the passage and into the back room. 'They were marvellous, didn't make any mess at all.'

'How did it catch light?'

'I was holding a newspaper over the fire, to draw it, but the wood was wet and the paper caught light. It shot straight up the chimney.'

'It was ever so smoky, Daddy,' Corinne chirped excitedly. 'We had to go out in the street and Mrs Spicer took me to the sweet shop and bought me some sweets.' To this day, Corinne's only recourse to memory retrieval is by way of food recognition.

Ray and his wife from a few doors along poked their heads into the open street door. 'Everything okay?'

'Yeah, we're fine, thanks.'

'Nosey buggers.'

'No they're not! they're really nice people – don't be a miserable sod,' retorted Joan. She was right of course; it was a really nice neighbourhood – rows of terraced houses not unlike St James's Road, where people shared in each others' trials and tribulations.

'Come in, Ray,' I shouted.

'Bit of excitement for the street, Jim!'

Ray's wife Pat pulled up a dining room chair and took up residence in front of the television. 'Emergency Ward 10. I love this. I bet that little blonde nurse has it away with that dishy doctor.' She had barely finished the sentence when the picture fused down to a white horizontal line and went black.

'Sod it, we haven't got any sixpencees,' said Joan, fishing through her purse. Ray looked puzzled. 'It's a slot telly,' I explained. 'Saves us having to find a lump at the end of the month.' Ray agreed it was a 'bloody good idea' as he emptied his pocket in search of a sixpence. 'Nope,' he shook his head dejectedly. 'Oh well, as long as you're all okay,' Pat said hurriedly as she jumped up from the chair, grabbed Ray's arm and made her exit back to number 299.

I closed the front door behind them, walked back into the back room, pulled a sixpenny piece from my pocket and turned the winged spindle on the slot meter. 'You rotten cowson.' I slumped into the armchair and smiled as Joan jumped into my lap.

★

I was halfway down the fifty foot escape ladder with Chris Tisi on my back when the yard bells summoned us to our next shout. 'Knock off, make up,' shouted the leading fireman, 'And make it snappy. Persons reported.'

I started to descend the ladder at a much increased pace.

'Step in,' shouted Daisy a little belatedly as I missed my footing on the lower extension. 'Ugh,' moaned Chris as he bounced back on to my shoulders, 'Take it easy, Jim.' We hurriedly made all the gear up on the PE, whilst the pump burst through the open bay doors and sped towards Manbey Park Grove.

'Isn't that where you live, Chris?' He nodded anxiously. As we turned into the Grove, Chris breathed a sigh of relief. The job was at the far end. The pump had already set into a hydrant; the thirty foot extension ladder had been pitched to the first floor window of the three-storey building. The lower floor was below street level and seemed unaffected by the fire as did the ground floor.

Smoke was billowing out of the broken windows on the first floor. The premises were in multiple occupancy and therefore BA crews had already been committed to search the various floors. Docherty pulled my arm and dragged me towards the smoke-filled building. Here we go again, I thought to myself, no bloody sets, he's going smoke eating. We ran up the concrete steps that led to the ground floor entrance door, passing a large West Indian gentleman coughing and carrying a television set out of the house. 'Everybody out, chief?' enquired the sub-officer.

'No man, de wife's upstairs somewhere!'

Docherty shook his head in total disbelief. We bounded up the wooden staircase to the first floor. Visibility was down to practically zero. At least the doors off the landing were closed; searching in the rooms should be relatively easy.

'You take that room Jim; I'll take this one.' I must be going up in the sub-officers estimation; he rarely referred to me by my Christian name. I knelt down in front of the bedroom door and placed the back of my hand on one of the inlaid panels. It was warm but not hot. Crouching down, I shielded myself to one side of the door as I gently opened it. The smoke in the corridor wafted past me and into the cooler room. Coughing, I edged cautiously forward into the bedroom.

'Don't touch me, don't touch me,' screamed a woman's voice from the corner of the room. I stood bolt upright, spun round and found myself face to face with a huge black woman, stark naked and frantically waving her arms at me as if to stop my approach. 'You not goin' t'carry me down no ladder, man.' I tried to take in the enormity of her suggestion – she must have weighed about twenty stone. Her large breasts lifted and dropped back on to her belly as she jumped up and down excitedly, gesturing me away.

'You're bloody right, darlin', we're not going down the ladder, we're going down the stairs. Put this around you.' I grabbed the large eiderdown off the bed to cover her up. She wrapped it around her and, gripping the two edges together at her back, proceeded in front of me towards the stairs. 'Let me go in front, luv, it's a bit smoky.' Apart from the fact that we had been taught to assist people downstairs in this fashion, I didn't fancy the sight of the lady's exposed buttocks in my face all the way downstairs anyway.

'I see Hooligan's found 'imself a new bint.' The flattened nose and puffed eyebrows of Vic Evans greeted me along with the grinning crew from Plaistow's pump, who had been ordered on with Silvertown's pump at the time of the make-up.

'You're too bloody late again,' Chris Rumford said in a mocking, yet triumphant tone. 'What kept you, Paddy?'

Station Officer McGinty shrugged his shoulders in a gesture of defeat. The large black woman called frantically after her husband. 'Get me some clothes, you bastard, you tink more of de telly dan you do of me.' We established that she was not hurt and she didn't want to go to hospital. Her husband was eventually allowed to re-enter the house to clothe his unfortunate wife.

'I hear you're into racing pigeons now, Paddy,' said Chris Rumford, who had obviously heard the rumour about McGinty's latest disaster. Paddy apparently sent away to the North East of England the sum of twelve pounds in order to purchase a champion homing pigeon, which was duly dispatched to him by rail.

'I can't make it out, yer know, I gave it a little fly round and I ain't seen the bloody fing since, four bleedin' weeks ago that was!' The guy who sold it to poor old Paddy must be making a fortune with that bird.

We made our gear up on the PE and left the pump to await the arrival of the London Salvage Corps. The Salvage Corps were a fleet of tenders, looking somewhat like our hose-laying lorries and manned by officers wearing fire gear similar to our own. They were financed by the insurance companies. Their duties were to prevent further damage to contents and structure from the effects of the fire and water.

We had just turned into Water Lane when we received a call on the radio to release a person who was shut in a lift. We pulled up outside the block of flats in West Ham Lane, 'Daisy, Chris; you two go upstairs to the lift motor room,' ordered Docherty. 'O'Halloran, you grab the lift keys and come with me.'

'She's stuck between the ninth and tenth floors,' shouted the caretaker as we ran past him and up the stone stairway. We reached the tenth floor panting for breath.

Woodsie and Chris Tisi grabbed the handrail, pulled themselves wearily to the nineteenth floor and entered the lift motor room. Their first priority was to immobilise the power supply to the lift, then connect a large iron wheel handle to the main spindle of the lift pulley mechanism. Once this was done they could then release the brake mechanism with a large iron lever that hung in the motor room. The pump's crew had now arrived to assist. Crew members were placed at varying floors between the tenth and the top to relay instructions. Docherty juggled with the assortment of keys on the steel ring, searching for the correct one. Each lift manufacturer, for some reason, developed their own lift key and mechanism. We therefore had to carry the lot. A universal key would have been the answer. The sub-officer poked the half-circled steel key into the lift door lock.

'Hello, can you hear me?' I shouted at the closed doors. 'Hello?' There was a prolonged silence, then a slight whimpering.

'Hello,' came the reply through staggered sobs.

'We'll soon have you out. What's your name?'

There was more uncontrollable crying. 'Tracey,' came the reply.

'How old are you Tracey?'

'S-s-s-six.'

'Don't cry, be a brave girl.'

'Bloody thing's useless.' Docherty dragged the key from the lock in frustration. 'Get me a crowbar off the pump, Tom.' The caretaker looked anxiously at Docherty.

'What are you going to do?'

'Get the bloody doors open,' retorted the sub-officer.

'Shh, shh.' I placed my ear against the door.

'Hello,' the little voice cried.

'It's all right, Tracey, we're still here,' I tried to reassure the little girl.

'What's your name?' she asked.

'Jim.'

There was a long silence, then she continued, 'If I die, will you tell my mummy I love her.'

As I looked at Jim Docherty I swear his eyes started to water; I know mine were. I blinked hard to disguise my emotion.

'You're not going to die, silly, you'll be with your mummy shortly.' Her sobbing increased as our frantic efforts to open the doors were turning to panic.

'The keys won't open the doors on the ninth, either,' said Fireman Delarue as he hurried to join us. 'Put some pressure on this crowbar, O'Halloran.' I grabbed the bar and pushed as Docherty applied all his strength in an effort to force the doors apart. There was a loud echoing crack as the doors finally succumbed, much to the caretaker's horror. We peered down the shaft and could see the top of the lift. 'It's all right, Tracey, nearly there now, love.' The calls to wind the lift slowly to the tenth were relayed up the escape stairs. 'The top of the lift edged its way past the floor. I peered through the ever-increasing gap and got my first glimpse of the terrified little girl huddled in one corner. I squeezed through the gap and jumped down into the lift.

'Come on, Tracey, it's all over now, no need for any more tears.'

'Stop winding,' shouted Chris Rumford. I picked the curly-headed blonde child up in my arms and wiped her reddened cheeks with my black silk.

'You smell all smoky,' she said, as though deeply disappointed by her rescuer. I smiled at her quizzical expression.

'Oh dear, I'm terribly sorry, young lady, but I had to put a fire out before I came to see you.' She seemed to accept my explanation with some reluctance as I passed her through the enlarged gap and into the arms of her anxious mother who had just arrived.

'His name's Jim,' she said to her mother admiringly. 'He got me out.'

Daisy clasped my shoulder. 'My *hero*.'

As we drove back to the station, Daisy pulled the huge book he had been reading from under the seat and thumbed the pages towards the back. His puzzled look remained on his face for a few seconds. 'That rotten sod!'

'Who, what are you talking about?'

'Evans, that's who. He's cut the last page out.'

We arrived back at the station, scrubbed and washed the hose and hung it in the drill tower to dry. The little girl was right; I did smell of smoke. I decided to have a quick shower. As my clothes had got quite wet at Manby Park Grove, I took them across the corridor to the drying room. I stripped off, wrapped a towel around my waist and dashed back to the shower room. My urgency to cross the corridor was because Stratford was now the Eastern Command, and a new central control room had been constructed in what was one of the front offices. It was largely manned by women and these ladies used the corridor to reach the upstairs mess. Having showered, I retraced my steps across the corridor, gripping the towel around my waist. Fireman Tisi, following behind me, snatched the towel and dived back behind the locker room door, which was duly slammed and locked instantly.

'The little wop bastard,' I muttered under my breath as I tried vainly to force the door open. I could hear the idle female chatter emanating from the now open door of the control room as the girls prepared to go to the mess. Back to the drying room! It seemed a logical conclusion at the time. I bounced off the locked door as I tried valiantly to gain entry. I could here the triumphant cries of my 'mates' from behind the door. Running upstairs was not an option, and as all other routes appeared to be blocked I decide to brave it out defiantly. I marched proudly towards them, smiled and bade them 'good afternoon ladies', much to their amusement; as Joan said, little things please little minds. I was greeted ecstatically, like some returning conquering hero, by my watch.

It was two weeks later, on our first night shift, that I attended my second twenty-pump fire. We were ordered on to a ship alight in the Royal Victoria Dock. As we made our way over the Canning Town bypass we could clearly see a huge pool of black smoke swirling above the cranes in the dock.

'It's a goer,' shouted Tom from the back of the pump. 'Better get rigged in BA.' Because of the number of engines stacked up along the quayside, we parked some two hundred yards away from the listing, stricken vessel. I struggled to put my head harness on as we criss-crossed our way over the maze of twisted lengths of hose that led to the ship. Plaistow's PE crew were sitting dejectedly on some barrels on the dockside, still wearing their exhausted BA sets. The black grimy foreheads and cheeks highlighted the white rings around their eyes which had been protected by their goggles.

'It's a total balls up,' muttered Vic Evans. 'That lot know sod all about boats!' He gestured towards a group of senior officers huddled together with what appeared to be a plan of the ship. 'They've 'ad it upside bleedin' down, side bleedin' ways and corner to bleedin' corner. Ain't got a clue!'

In all probability, it would have been the first experience of a fire aboard ship for most of these London officers, and unfortunately those that did have the expertise, like Cutting and Baker, were off duty.

Silvertown's crew emerged from the bowels of the ship, sweating profusely and covered in thick black oily grime.

'Christ it's 'ot down there, can't see a bloody fing,' mumbled Paddy McGinty as he wrestled to unbuckle the straps on his BA set. 'Half of this lot shit themselves when they got down there.'

As we made our way to the BA entry point that led to the ship's engine room, there were mumblings from other crews that some teams had only been in the first fifty yards or so and had then deliberately emptied their sets of air in order to return to the surface, whilst other crews had already been in twice.

'Okay, down you go.' The BA control officer had checked the contents of my cylinder and taken my tag. 'Follow the hose and the main BA guideline to the engine room.' Paddy was right; the intense heat hit us almost immediately as we stepped over the bulkhead doorstop. I thrust my hand forward through the blackness, searching for the metal handrail. 'Christ, that's hot,' I mumbled through my mouthpiece, as my hand recoiled from the rail. The heat had scorched my debris glove. Daisy and Chris followed me cautiously down the metal stairs, as we edged past various crews making their way back to the surface. We had nearly reached the third level when a loud whooshing noise roared towards us from the bowels of the engine room, followed by a thunderous explosion. The force of the blast initially lifted me backwards into my two companions, knocking them over and then somersaulting me forwards down the stairs and on to the metal floor. The deafening noise of the explosion slowly abated to a rumble. All was still except for the constant rolling of my helmet on the floor. I lay there dazed as the rumble faded into total silence. Oh, Christ Almighty, here we go again!

Home Alone

Before I know what's happening I'm leaping out of bed;
I slip shoes on to my feet, there's ringing in my head.
With heart jumping out of chest I try hard to control
The feelings and emotions that affect body and soul.

The bells ring on, the lights are bright, I quickly look
    around:
The dormitory now alive, and still the ringing sound;
I'm making for the sliding pole, crash through the safety
    doors
And clinging none too tightly, I'm whisked down to lower
    floors.

Once in the bay, into the pump, start putting on my gear,
No more an automaton and at last I'm thinking clear.
The guv'nor mounts and shouts the news: a house fire,
    people trapped;
It's Guy Fawkes night, our fifteenth call, and energy is
    sapped.

We gaze out from the windows at the houses flashing by;
The blue light helps us on our way as through the streets
    we fly.
Instructions passing to and fro, the driver needs to know
The street, the number of the house, exactly where to go.

As always when there's life involved, we double-check our
    gear;
Each man is silent with his thoughts, with little hint of fear.
Adrenaline now starts to flow, somehow we must succeed,
Our thoughts with those who may be trapped and
    desperately in need.

Our breathing apparatus donned, we're ready for the fire;
Subconciously we build our strength, the situation dire.
The driver shouts, he's seen the smoke: back to reality.
A crowd has gathered by the house, outside a casualty.

Although she's burnt and on the floor, her cry for help is
    strong;
She's calling for her baby, and why have we been so long?
No time to argue: 'Where?' we ask, 'What bedroom is it in?'
'She's in the box room in the back.' She then breaks down,
    crying.

I turn round; Jimbo's disappeared, he's halfway up the
    stairs.
A hose-reel's shoved into my hand, I follow like a hare.
The smoke is dense, some stairs have gone; with backs
    close to the wall,
We make our way on to the landing; then we hear the call.

'Mummy!' she cries, and suddenly – relief – experience
    tells
It's not the scream of pain we hear, but out of fear she yells.
The bedroom door is black and blistered, the heat is now
    intense;
Thank God the door was tightly shut: at least that showed
good sense.

We burst into the room and there she lies, a child all alone;
She's swooped up into Jimbo's arms, he holds her like his
    own:
And now the only thought in mind is to get out with all
    haste;
The stairs have finally burnt away, there's no more time to
    waste.

To the window, glory be, the lads have done their bit;
The ladder's propped against the sill and soon we're out of
    it.
Straight to the ambulance Jimbo goes, to place the child
    within:
Not that she's hurt, but Mum's inside and gives a loving
    grin.

We share the moment with them both, and then we have to
    turn;
It seems the smoke that's in our eyes has cause to make
    them burn.
I look at Jim and wonder if he thinks the same as me,
And turning to the woman ask a question tenderly.

I ask her where her husband is, why is he not at home?
What kind of man, on Guy Fawkes night, leaves his family
    alone?
She whispers that he has no choice, his job he will not
    shirk;
You see, he's just a fireman, and he sometimes has to work.

Ken Smith